TOMORROW'S CITIZENS

Critical debates in citizenship and education

edited by Nick Pearce and
Joe Hallgarten

30-32 Southampton St
London WC2E 7RA
Tel: 0171 470 6100
Fax: 0171 470 6111
postmaster@ippr.org.uk
www.ippr.org.uk
Registered charity 800065

The Institute for Public Policy Research is an independent charity whose purpose is to contribute to public understanding of social, economic and political questions through research, discussion and publication. It was established in 1988 by leading figures in the academic, business and trade-union communities to provide an alternative to the free market think tanks.

IPPR's research agenda reflects the challenges facing Britain and Europe. Current programmes cover the areas of economic and industrial policy, Europe, governmental reform, human rights, defence, social policy, the environment and media issues.

Besides its programme of research and publication, IPPR also provides a forum for political and trade union leaders, academic experts and those from business, finance, government and the media, to meet and discuss issues of common concern.

Trustees

Production & design by **EMPHASIS**
Cover design by PUSH
ISBN 1 86030 096 0

Contents

Acknowledgements

The IPPR wishes to acknowledge the generous support of OCR, Evans & WH Smith for making possible this publication and the conference on which its papers are based. Particular thanks go to Melissa Bullock, Maxine Vlieland, Jenny Fowler, and to Raymond Plant and Malcolm Wicks MP, for their contributions to the original conference event. The editors would also like to thank Rachel Lissauer, Carey Oppenheim, Helena Scott and Sarah Spencer of the IPPR for their invaluable editorial assistance. Final responsibility naturally rests with the editors alone.

Foreword

This book started life as a set of papers given at a conference held by the Institute for Public Policy Research in June 1999 to examine contemporary concepts of citizenship and their implications for education. Our purpose in holding the conference was to enrich public debate at a time when the government had opened consultation on the future shape of the National Curriculum, and, in particular, on the proposed new place within it of citizenship education.

In a significant development in education policy, the government has decided that citizenship education should be introduced into the school curriculum in England with effect from 2002. Citizenship will become a new statutory foundation subject in secondary schools, and part of the non-statutory framework in primary schools, alongside personal, social and health education. These proposals build upon the conclusions of an Advisory Group on Citizenship, commissioned by Rt Hon David Blunkett MP, the Secretary of State for Education and Employment, and chaired by Professor Bernard Crick. Its landmark report, *Education for Citizenship and the Teaching of Democracy in Schools*, outlined a cogent and compelling case for statutory citizenship education.[1]

In many edited collections, authors write in isolation. The strength of this book is that the speakers were able to engage in each other's arguments at the conference. The book has been structured to demonstrate this jigsaw of ideas. Broadly, the contributions move from the general to the specific; *Tomorrow's Policy* gives an overview of how the book's contributors interact with the broader current educational climate and wider philosophical debates. *Tomorrow's World* places concepts of citizenship in the context of 'the big picture', the local and global forces shaping our society. *Tomorrow's Citizens* relates these forces more directly to the world of education. *Tomorrow's Practice* adds *realpolitik* to the debate, grounding the arguments in current realities, both positive and challenging.

The contributions aim to be accessible to both the deliverers and the consumers of citizenship education. Citizenship arguments lie at the heart of much of IPPR's work in all policy areas. As with all of our projects, it is hoped that the publication marks not an end but a continuation of active engagement with the ideas expressed. As a 'listening think tank' we would welcome constructive criticism of the book. We look forward to hearing from you.

Matthew Taylor
Director
Institute for Public Policy Research

1 Advisory Group on Citizenship (1998) *Education for Citizenship and the Teaching of Democracy in Schools* London: Qualifications and Curriculum Authority

About the Contributors

Professor Anthony Giddens has been Director of the LSE since 1997, having previously been Professor of Sociology and fellow of King's College Cambridge.

He is internationally famous for his writings in the areas of sociology, politics and social theory. He is the author or editor of more than 30 books, which have been translated into as many languages. Among recent books are *The Consequences of Modernity* (1989), *Modernity and Self Identity* (1991), *The Transformation of Intimacy* (1992), *Beyond Left and Right* (1994), *In Defence of Sociology* (1996), and *The Third Way: The Renewal of Social Democracy* (1998). He is the author of *Sociology*, the leading introductory text in the subject. In 1999 he was BBC Reith Lecturer. He is also a director of Polity Press, a leading publisher in the social sciences and humanities.

David Miller is an Official Fellow in Social and Political Theory at Nuffield College, Oxford. He has written extensively on the subjects of nationality, citizenship and democracy.

His books include *On Nationality* (1995), *Principles of Social Justice* (1999) and *Citizenship and National Identity* (1999).

Professor Anne Phillips is a Professor in Gender Theory at the LSE, as well as the Director of the Gender Institute. She was previously Professor of Politics at London Guildhall University

Her publications include *Democracy and Difference* (Polity Press, 1992), *The Politics of Presence* (1995), and *Which Equalities Matter?* (1999)

Stuart Hall is an Emeritus Professor of the Open University. He was Research Fellow, then Director, of The Centre for Cultural Studies, University of Birmingham, from 1964-79. From 1979-97 he was Professor of Sociology, The Open University, and is a former President of the British Sociological Association. Currently he is Chair of the Institute for the International Visual Arts and the Association of Black Photography, a member of the Runnymede Commission on the Future of Multi-ethnic Britain, and Visiting Professor, Goldsmiths College, University of London, since 1997. He is Founder-Editor of *New Left Review*.

Rabbi Professor Jonathan Sacks has been Chief Rabbi of the United Hebrew Congregations of the Commonwealth since September 1991. He was previously Principal of Jews' College, London, where he also held the Chair of Modern Jewish Thought.

Professor Sacks has been Visiting Professor of Philosophy at the University of Essex, Sherman Lecturer at Manchester University, Riddell Lecturer at Newcastle University, and Cook Lecturer at the Universities of Oxford, Edinburgh and St Andrews. In 1997 he delivered the first Yerusha (Jewish Heritage) Lecture at Cambridge University. During 1998 he became Visiting Professor of the Hebrew University, Jerusalem and King's College, London.

He is a frequent contributor to radio, televison and the national press; in 1990 he delivered the BBC Reith Lectures on *The Persistance of Faith*. His books include *Tradition in an Untraditional Age* (1990), *Crisis and Covenant* (1992), *Faith in the Future* (1995), and *The Politics of Hope* (1997).

Dr Nicholas Tate has been Chief Executive of the Qualifications and Curriculum Authority (QCA) since its establishment in October 1997. QCA's responsibilities cover all aspects of curriculum, assessment and qualifications from the under fives to higher level vocational qualifications.

Dr Tate was previously Chief Executive of the School Curriculum and Assessment Authority (SCAA) and, before that, worked for both the School Examinations and Assessment Council and the National Curriculum Council. His earlier career involved experience in schools and colleges in England and Scotland, with examination boards, with the Open University, and as author of many textbooks. In September 2000, Dr Tate will take up a new post as Headmaster of Winchester College.

Professor Bernard Crick is Emeritus Professor of Politics, Birkbeck College, author of *In Defence of Politics* and of *George Orwell: a Life*; chairman of the advisory committee on Education for Citizenship and the Teaching of Democracy in Schools that reported in 1998. He is currently an adviser to the DFEE on citizenship.

Charles Clarke MP is Minister of State at the Home Office. From July 1998 until July 1999, he was Parliamentary Under Secretary of State for

School Standards, where his responsibilities included the National Curriculum Review, including PSHE and Citizenship.

He entered politics as a researcher to Neil Kinnock, and became his chief of staff from 1983-92. From 1992-97 he was Chief Executive of Quality Public Affairs, a public affairs management consultancy, before being elected as Member of Parliament for Norwich South.

Jenny Talbot was appointed Chief Executive of the Institute for Citizenship in January 1997. She has spent 18 years campaigning, and working in project and financial management in the public and voluntary sectors. She has worked in both a front-line and senior management capacity and co-founded Common Purpose, a national charity, in 1988.

Coventry University awarded her the Honary Degree of MA in 1993 in recognition of pioneering work and outstanding contributions to community leadership and development.

In 1993 she completed an MBA, with the thesis on Corporate Social Responsibility, at De Montfort University. She is also a Fellow of the Royal Society of Arts.

William Atkinson has been Head of Phoenix High School in Hammersmith and Fulham LEA since 1995, having previously held headships at Cranford Community School, Brent. He is a member of the DfEE Standards Task Force, and of the Preparation for Life Group (QCA). He has recently been on the Home Office Youth Justice Task Force and the DfEE Special Measures Action Recovery Team.

He has contributed to a range of TV and radio programmes, including Newsnight, Panorama, Any Questions and You and Yours, and has had a variety of speaking engagements in England, Wales and Canada.

Martin Cross is Director-General of OCR (Oxford, Cambridge and RSA Examinations). He was a member of the Speaker's Commission on Citizenship, 1988-89. He has served on a number of Governmental advisory committees, and is currently Chair of the Joint Council for General Qualifications.

TOMORROW'S POLICY

What's new in citizenship education?

Nick Pearce and Joe Hallgarten

Introduction

Nick Pearce and Joe Hallgarten

Citizenship education: framing the debate

Amidst the fascinating tensions between the contributions to this book, an overwhelming consensus emerges: the Government's proposal that citizenship education should be included in the revised national curriculum is a positive step. This consensus – broadly, if not entirely, shared by education policymakers and practitioners – is perhaps surprising, since the proposal is a radical one. For it will be an historic shift in education policy if, at the beginning of the new century, a place can at last be found for citizenship within the school curriculum. As David Kerr has noted:

> the history of education for citizenship in England is a curious mixture of noble intentions, which are then turned into general pronouncements, which, in turn, become minimal guidance for schools. The avoidance of any overt official government direction to schools concerning political socialisation and citizenship education can almost be seen as a national trait. Such education has long been perceived as unbecoming, vulgar, and 'unEnglish'[1]

This deficit becomes even more stark when viewed from an international perspective. As David Miller points out, the concept of citizenship has a more problematic status in the United Kingdom than in many other democratic countries. The notion of the citizen is one with which we are uncomfortable and which we view as somehow alien to our political culture. This is unsurprising, given the absence of a written constitution, a history of citizenship rights, or a civic republican tradition of active self-government. The historical trajectory and political culture of the countries of the United Kingdom since the English civil war have mitigated against the idea of citizenship and the transmission through the education system of a set of civic values, purposes, skills and knowledge. This has left citizenship education at the margins of the school system, implicit in the curriculum if present at all, rather than explicit and clearly understood by teachers, parents and local communities.

This situation is now set to change. Democracy is undergoing a transformation and new forms of civic engagement are emerging in the United Kingdom. These include processes which Anthony Giddens identifies as the 'second wave of democratisation', and which can be seen at work in the renewal of democratic participation in the United Kingdom: devolution, the reinvention of local government, the development of new forms of deliberative or direct democracy, and the impact of new media on socialisation and democratic communication. All these forces promise to inject new urgency into the task of educating young people for citizenship.

Indeed, the disastrously low turnouts in the 1999 local government and European Parliament elections, as well as apparently muted enthusiasm for new forms of devolved political power in parts of the United Kingdom, form an ominous backdrop to this volume. Whether these represent a temporary trough or the sharpening of a trend towards lower voter turnout in mature democracies is a matter of debate. Either way, concern with what Bernard Crick's Advisory Group on Citizenship's report called the 'inexcusably and damagingly bad' state of political literacy amongst young people is high. This thread runs throughout the contributions.[2]

However, it is also a theme that is susceptible to 'golden-ageism'. Undoubtedly, there has been a rise in the numbers of young people who are disaffected from all forms of civic institutions, school, the neighbourhood, the family. Yet these still form a small minority of our school-age population. For the majority, engagement with mainstream politics may be weak, but involvement with the margins is flourishing; from single-issue activism, to participation in school councils and youth parliaments. Even the common cliché that young people 'know their rights too well' demonstrates their sophistication, expressed through an ability to challenge social norms. It's a form of political literacy, if not a traditional one.

Of course, education for citizenship is far more than what used to be known as 'civics'. The report of the Advisory Group on Citizenship offered a tripartite definition of citizenship education, covering social and moral responsibility, community involvement, and political literacy.

Citizenship education, the report argued, consists of the habitual interaction of these three.

We explore the meaning of this definition, and its implications, throughout this volume. Contributors also examine the political context within which discussions on citizenship education are currently framed. How we think about the rights and duties of citizenship, and the parameters of democracy, for example, are subject to extensive contemporary political debate. Citizenship education must face the challenges posed by this debate. Whilst it is clearly not a sufficient condition for the renewal of active citizenship in a healthy democracy, it is surely, as Bernard Crick argues, a necessary one.

The sections below describe how the book's contributors, and other thinkers, tackle these issues. Below the consensus that has emerged to support the value of citizenship education lie substantial and critical intellectual questions about the definition, purposes, and intended outcomes of such education.

What is a citizen?

What then, is this problematic thing, the citizen? David Miller's paper outlines three types of citizen: a liberal model in which rights and responsibilities are balanced to give all citizens equal status; a consumer model in which citizens' rights can be more actively expressed, if on an individual basis; and a third model, which involves collective civic engagement. If definitions of a citizen can be put on a sliding scale, from individual/passive to collective/active, then Miller would argue that the UK is somewhere in the middle.

Anne Phillips, on the other hand, asserts that citizenship in the UK may not have even achieved Miller's liberal model. Her paper examines how women and ethnic minorities have been the bearers of 'second-class citizenship', despite formal equality. The political problem Phillips poses is how claims of citizenship can be made by groups which assert different identities without freezing, and thereby consolidating, a notion of the normal to which those differences are posed as Other.

Conversely, anti-discrimination strategies, which promote equality of citizenship – or equal status despite difference – may render inconceivable or illegal positive discrimination, which relies upon conscious concern with such difference. Moreover, anti-discrimination may establish norms of what it means to receive equal treatment, and require those who are different to accept prevailing identities or practices.

This leaves a dilemma: equal citizenship needs to recognise and validate difference, but those differences may themselves need to be challenged. Phillips turns this dilemma into a 'healthy reminder' of an ongoing tension in citizenship discourses between the different and the normal.

Stuart Hall develops this theme of what he describes as 'the arrival of difference' in a multicultural context.[3] Concepts of the nation state in the UK have undergone a series of implosions and explosions, due to the forces of globalisation, the loss of empire and the increasing cultural diversity of its inhabitants. We may have been 'sleepwalking into diversity', but citizenship education must attempt to understand and articulate the multiple identities of an increasing number of our population.[4] William Atkinson's description of his own school's intake reaffirms the practical importance of Stuart Hall's theoretical framework. As Charles Clarke hints, schools in predominantly white areas have much to learn from the current practice of many multiracial inner city schools.

Citizenship, equality and democracy

For egalitarians, the healthy functioning of a democracy depends on the existence of what TH Marshall famously called the 'social rights' of citizenship: certain social conditions which are pre-requisites for equality in the exercise of the formal rights of citizenship[5]. Although Marshall notoriously failed to grasp the nettle of sexual equality, his thesis inspired an understanding of citizenship that implied not just formal but substantive equality. This understanding needs to be reinforced today, Phillips argues, since the social and economic conditions of citizenship have slipped out of sight in contemporary political discourses. Whilst tackling 'unfinished business around the political and civil rights of citizenship' has been the positive achievement of the last few decades, it is necessary to resurrect earlier concerns with convergence in material welfare, and to knit together (earlier) social and (later) political and civil discourses on citizenship.[6]

Another argument often made by egalitarians is that democracy cannot bear too much inequality before the social fabric begins to unravel. However, reductions in inequality require mutual commitment amongst members of a political community. Unless members of the community consider themselves citizens who share in a common social endeavour, the prospects for reducing inequality are thin. In particular, mutuality is necessary for explicitly redistributive policies.[7] Without mutual commitment, expressed in a framework of righs and duties, redistributive policies are likely to be overwhelmed by material interests, which count for more than social solidarity in the ballot box amongst key voting constituencies. The question is whether citizenship education should try to educate young people for a stronger form of commonality than currently appears to obtain in the UK, or just to produce citizens capable of addressing in the ballot box political arguments posed by democratic debate? In short, *how full is the content of civic identity?*

Citizenship, liberty and autonomy

At this point, citizenship debates usually confront a central argument posed by political philosophy. Chiefly, it is this: should a democracy embody a particular concept of ethical or good life of fundamental importance to communities – political, religious, philosophical or otherwise? Or should the state, and the conditions of citizenship it expresses in law, be neutral between competing concepts, securing instead an 'overlapping consensus' for plural democracy that sets out the rights and duties of citizenship but not the substantive ends that citizens should pursue?

This argument goes to the heart of the debate between liberalism and its communitarian critics. Many liberals argue for the priority of the right over the good. Individuals should be free to pursue different conceptions of substantive ethical life within a framework of fundamental rights and guaranteed liberties. These rights and liberties must be protected by the state and cannot be sacrificed to a general good or the welfare of others. The state must remain neutral between the substantive moral positions taken by individuals, only ruling out those that violate individual rights.

Communitarians have articulated forceful critiques of these basic tenets of rights-based liberalism. They criticise liberals for relying on disembodied, asocial and ultimately implausible understandings of individuals, as if people are somehow able to separate the ends they pursue from the communities that have shaped them. Moreover, liberal ethical neutrality reduces morality to the arbitrary and subjective choices of individuals, and consequently fails to offer a compelling account of what forms of human activity and social life are good and valuable. Individual free choice, elevated above the good of the community, corrodes the social fabric and the shared bonds of civil society. For many communitarian theorists, therefore, the legitimacy of the community as the repository of authority for social norms and as a site of collective self-government, must be restored to centrality in advanced capitalist democracies.

Much interesting recent political theory has been devoted to exploring the middle ground between liberal and communitarian concerns, or as Stuart Hall puts it, reconciling the right and the good. A perfectionist liberalism of the sort advocated by Joseph Raz, for example, seeks to combine freedom and pluralism with the pursuit of a core conception of the good life by placing human autonomy at the centre of liberal political philosophy.[8] For Raz, the state cannot be neutral. It must promote a specific concept of ethical life, albeit one that preserves moral pluralism. This is possible if the core ethical value is the pursuit of a genuinely autonomous life, which requires that individuals have a plurality of worthwhile and socially sustained options from which to choose and with which to shape their lives.

Common citizenship

In this sense, Raz's ethical liberalism is close to what Charles Taylor has called *holist individualism*: 'a trend of thought that is fully aware of the (ontological) social embedding of human agents, but at the same time prizes liberty and values individual differences very highly.'[9] It also echoes John Gray's plea, approvingly quoted by Dr Nick Tate in his contribution to this volume, for an individualism that is balanced by a strong public culture, moored in key institutions.

The government's proposals for citizenship education appear to fall into similar territory. To begin with, in a plural society of diverse beliefs and practices, citizenship education cannot offer one vision of what constitutes a good or moral life, unless that vision is itself a plural one. But it must educate people for engagement with the public good and broader civic virtues. Consequently, the report of the Advisory Group on Citizenship sought to place citizenship education within the context of a pluralist society that requires basic but robust civic and political foundations. A key passage in the report states:

> A main aim for the whole community should be to find or restore a sense of common citizenship, including a national identity that is secure enough to find a place for the plurality of nations, cultures, ethnic identities and religions long found in the United Kingdom. Citizenship education creates common ground between different ethnic and religious identities.[10]

Jonathan Sacks describes how Jewish history has provided its communities with a strong sense of such common citizenship, a reserve of active empathy that can be mobilised on behalf of other cultures and communities. Yet Sacks also points out that this can only be achieved through 'the reciprocal support of schools, families and communities.'[11] How far can schools forge a common citizenship if the social and economic forces outside the school gates are pulling in the opposite direction? To warp a famous phrase, *can schools, and the citizenship education they teach, compensate for society?*

British society is still recovering from two decades of policies predicated on the conviction that no social horizon exists beyond the individual or family. Inequalities in income, health, and educational performance are agreed to be the highest in Europe. Our culture has become more profoundly individualistic. If 'common citizenship' existed, would we have allowed the multiple factors that create social exclusion to build up? The success of citizenship education will then depend as much on the government's wider social and economic policies, as on the performance of teachers and schools.

Citizenship, rights and responsibilities

For Nick Tate, it is clear that the objective of common citizenship requires a stronger emphasis on duties and social obligations than is currently the case. As he points out, liberalism is not libertarianism. Citizenship education is about the cultivation of civic virtues for a society that refuses to succumb to moral relativism. But this does not mean abandoning individual rights; indeed the reverse. As Richard Dagger points out in his book, *Civic Virtues*, the development of a republican or civic liberalism which reconciles the pursuit of individual autonomy with the cultivation of civic responsibility and common purpose:

> ...does not mean abandoning our concern for rights. We could not do that if we wanted to, for the concept of rights is too deeply engrained in our thinking simply to be abandoned. Nor *should* we want to even if we could. There is too much of value in the idea of rights – an idea rooted in firm and widespread convictions about human dignity and equality – to forsake it. The task, instead, is to find a way of strengthening the appeal of duty, community, and related concepts while preserving the appeal of rights.[12]

Realising such a task in complex societies is far from straightforward. Anthony Giddens's panoramic analysis of the transformations taking place in the global economy paints a picture of identities in flux, of the emergence of societies in which risk is constitutive, and of acute challenges to existing forms of governance. Charles Clarke describes how these transformations have rendered notions of citizenship both more crucial and more difficult to pinpoint. Developing communality of purpose in such rapidly changing and pluralising societies, whose values, beliefs and practices continue to multiply, will stretch the civic capacities of citizens and other social agencies to their limits. These complexities and insecurities increase the challenge to maintain belief in fundamental human rights, and increase the need to ensure their protection.

There is an urgency to this issue in the UK, since the 1998 Human Rights Act, which will come into force in October 2000, requires government and public authorities to act in a way which is compatible with the rights in the European Convention on Human Rights and gives individuals the right to seek a remedy in the court if they fail to do so. The Act is not simply about the introduction of new legal remedies for individuals, however, but much more broadly about a new culture of citizenship in which people and public authorities are guided by the principles of human rights, and importantly, by the duties and obligations those rights entail. Consequently, it provides significant new challenges for citizenship education.

Citizens of what?

The liberal/communitarian axis also impinges on our understanding of the political communities of which we are citizens. Crudely, communitarians are more likely to favour smaller communities with which people can actively and patriotically identify and to which they can give their energies as self-governing citizens. Those liberals, socialists and others for whom concepts of justice are universally valid are more likely to look beyond the local or particular community towards the global for the ultimate determination of the boundaries of citizenship.

The relevance of these questions has been sharpened by debates over shifts in forms of governance in the contemporary global economy, particularly in respect of the roles and powers of the nation state. Theorists of globalisation assert that global economic, social and cultural forces have swept away the capacity of the nation state to determine the basic conditions of existence within its territorial boundaries. As Anthony Giddens asserts, economic globalisation has deprived the nation state of its ability to manage the economy, whilst new problems, such as environmental pollution, do not respect arbitrary national boundaries and call for supra-national decision making bodies. Meanwhile, pressures for democratic renewal have led to the devolution of powers from the central nation state to local or regional bodies, sometimes, like Scotland or Wales, themselves formed on the basis of a constituent national identity. Simply stated, the power and authority, which rested at a national level have been ceded downwards to local democratic bodies and upwards to supra-national bodies, hollowing out the core of the nation state.

These claims are highly contested. Nonetheless, they are critical to debates on the future of citizenship education. If the nation state can no longer claim exclusive or even extensive sovereignty over its domain, then should we not educate young people for local civic engagement and European identity, rather than membership of a national polity? This, of course, is precisely what most European Union member states have sought to do.

David Miller's chapter takes issue with this argument. He argues that the nation state remains the key bearer of political identity and civic membership. The nation-state and, more particularly, national political identity, took centuries to develop. It is unlikely, Miller argues, that a European political or popular identity secure enough to form the basis of robust active citizenship can emerge in anything other than a period of decades, and perhaps far longer. For Miller, the nation state will remain the primary vehicle of political citizenship in the foreseeable future.

The response to this objection to European Union political citizenship has been eloquently put by Jurgen Habermas, who argues that:

> ...peoples come into being only with their state constitutions. Democracy itself is a juridically mediated form of political integration. Of course, democracy depends, in its turn, on the existence of a political culture shared by all citizens. But there is no call for defeatism, if one bears in mind that, in the nineteenth century European states, national consciousness and social solidarity were only gradually produced, with the help of national historiography, mass communications and universal conscription. If that artificial form of 'solidarity amongst strangers' came about thanks to a historically momentous effort of abstraction from local, dynastic consciousness, then why should it be impossible to extend this learning process beyond national borders?[13]

Habermas admits major hurdles to this process, noting that a critical precondition of the development of European identity is that European school systems give citizens a common grounding in foreign languages. But if the requisite constitutional, political and civil transformations take place, Habermas argues, then a common European political culture can be forged. However, a particularist Europe concerned only to establish a global bloc capable of competing with the USA would be morally objectionable. To avoid this scenario becoming the terminus of European integration, the capacity of transnational global institutions must be extended, in the absence of a global government, to facilitate a global 'domestic' politics. The long-term aim, Habermas argues, 'would have to be the gradual elimination of social divisions and stratification of world society without prejudice to cultural specificity.'[14]

Habermas's universalism has a rich heritage. As Seneca wrote, 'we measure the boundaries of our nation by the sun'.[15] Yet a universal perspective is not emptied of particular or local identity, and the citizenship curriculum must continually hold these in balance if a richer civic culture is to develop.

A character in O Henry's *The Four Million* typifies this dilemma.[16] He begins a bar room monologue, claiming that he is a citizen of the world, that he never feels American, that he forms no opinions when people tell him that they are Italian, Irish, or Indian. Yet five minutes later he is thrown out of the bar for starting a fight about whether the Yankees are better than the Giants. Running alongside our multiple identities are multiple loyalties, familial, local, national and global. Our senses of belonging form a set of intersecting circles, not subsets.

Citizenship education, schools and communities

As a new development in largely unchartered terrain, citizenship education poses many challenges for schools. Considerable professional and practical preparation needs to be undertaken for it to be introduced into schools successfully. For this reason, the government has delayed its implementation until 2002.

Citizenship education holds out a challenge to those who view children simply as subjects of instruction and whose concepts of discipline and school ethos cannot embrace forms of pupil participation and engagement. As Charles Clarke and Bernard Crick make clear, schools must practice what they preach if citizenship education is to be effective. The report of the Advisory Group on Citizenship strongly endorsed the need for schools to consider the relationship between their ethos, organisation and daily practices, particularly pupil discussion and consultation forums, and the aims and purposes of citizenship education. Schools must become, as Charles Clarke puts it, 'listening schools.'[17] Citizenship education is unlikely to mean much to pupils unless they are simultaneously engaged in participation in school decision-making and discussion procedures. Indeed, such pupil engagement is important to schooling more broadly, as studies of behaviour policies have shown.

Additionally, children and young adults may not be full political citizens until they reach voting age, but they are nonetheless citizens with rights, and for that matter, duties. Consequently, citizenship education cannot be considered entirely a matter of *preparation* for engagement in adult civil society, rather than something of value in itself. Citizenship education can improve the lives and school experiences of young people, and not just through spin-off effects on attainment in other subject areas. It is valuable for children as children.

The process by which governments, schools and individuals define citizenship is unlikely always to be consensual. One of the challenges for citizenship education will be to navigate a course through often-explosive political and cultural disagreement. The Advisory Group on Citizenship's report analyses how classroom teachers should handle issues likely to provoke controversy and disagreement, particularly when bias is unavoidable. But it demonstrates that painful choices will often have to be made in the teaching of citizenship that cannot be decanted into neutralised arenas. For example, can young people learn moral and social responsibility if they are not taught that all their fellow citizens are of equal worth, including those of different religious persuasions, sexual orientations, and so on? Here we are taken back rapidly to the dilemmas posed by Anne Phillips and Stuart Hall.

The Advisory Group's report also acknowledges that there are problems in teaching controversial subjects, but points out that citizenship education is not unique on this score. Issues of political significance arise frequently in subjects such as history, geography and religious education. This serves to remind us, if we needed reminding, that the curriculum is not a neutral thing, somehow extricated from its social and political context.

The converse is that citizenship education, as noted previously, should equip individuals for active engagement with the social and political lives of their communities, whether through formal democratic channels, or through autonomous public spaces in civil society. Citizenship education, in other words, should help to develop a more vibrant, robust and pluralised political culture. This is a critical role, for as Grefath puts it, a culture without thorns settles over risk society like a foam carpet.[18]

Will education for citizenship 'work'?

Compared to its previous inclusion as a cross curricular theme in the original National Curriculum, the new Order has been introduced by the government with enthusiasm and rigour. Yet schools and students must take up the challenge, rather than merely 'go through the citizenship motions'. In an era of targets and accreditation, a central factor may be the way in which citizenship education will be monitored and assessed. In his contribution to this volume Martin Cross argues that a citizenship GCSE and A Level could give the subject immediate status with pupils, parents and the general public.

Another factor will be the quality of teaching and resources allocated to citizenship education. As the consumers of the citizenship curriculum, students will be the ultimate arbiters of its popularity and success. Unless the subject is well taught (possibly by specialists), well resourced, and given constant 'relevance MOTs', citizenship education will always be in danger of becoming the 'truancy period' for 21st century pupils.

As William Atkinson points out, schools will embrace citizenship education with enthusiasm, if a little trepidation, but they will need practical support to do so effectively. This support must come in large measure from the communities of which they are a part: schools are critical institutions of civic life, and need better to be sustained by the social capital around them. Equally, however, the challenges they face – poverty in parental homes, high pupil turnover rates, weakened social norms – must be duly recognised in central and local government policy.

There are many fine examples of citizenship projects and activities in schools and their communities throughout the country, as Jenny Talbot and Charles Clarke outline. These examples will be important in helping teachers and schools unfamiliar with citizenship education to manage its introduction effectively. However, a healthy citizenship curriculum, just like a healthy civic society, will establish itself in multiple forms, with multiple identities. The advisory group and the Department for Education and Employment have avoided content overload and overprescription, creating a 'light touch' citizenship curriculum. The QCA, local authorities and Ofsted must similarly promote excellence whilst preventing a 'tyranny of best practice'. With such a new subject, schools must be free to prioritise their own values, to plan creatively, to take risks that may not always be successful. If they are able to innovate and excite, citizenship education will finally flourish.

Endnotes

1 Kerr, D (1999) *Re-examining citizenship education: the case of England* Slough: National Foundation for Educational Research

2 Advisory Group on Citizenship (1998) *Education for Citizenship and the Teaching of Democracy in Schools* London: Qualifications and Curriculum Authority p16. For a review of the report, see Pearce, N and Spencer, S 'Education for Citizenship: the Crick Report' *Political Quarterly* Vol 70, no 2, April-June 1999 p16

3 Hall, S 'Multicultural Citizens, Monocultural Citizenship?' in this volume

4 *ibid*

5 Marshall, TH (1950) *Citizenship and Social Class* Cambridge: Cambridge University Press

6 Phillips, A 'Second Class Citizenship' in this volume

7 For a short exposition of this argument, see Taylor, C 'Why Democracy Needs Patriotism' in Cohen, J (ed) (1996) *For Love of Country: Debating the Limits of Patriotism* Boston: Beacon Press

8 Raz, J (1986) *The Morality of Freedom* Oxford: Oxford University Press

9 Taylor, C 'Cross Purposes: The Liberal-Communitarian Debate' in Rosenblum, N (ed) (1989) *Liberalism and the Moral Life* Cambridge MA: Harvard University Press

10 Advisory Group on Citizenship *op cit* p17

11 Sacks J 'The Judaic Vision of Citizenship Education' in this volume

12 Dagger, R (1997) *Civic Virtues: Rights, Citizenship, and Republican Liberalism* Oxford: Oxford University Press p58

13 Habermas, J 'The European Nation State and the Pressures of Globalization' *New Left Review* no 235, May/June 1999 p58

14 *ibid*

15 Quoted in Cohen, J (ed) (1996) *For Love of Country: Debating the Limits of Patriotism* Boston: Beacon Press

16 Henry, O (1906) 'A Cosmopolite in a Café' in *The Four Million* New York: Mclure, Phillips & Co

17 Clarke C 'Creating Listening Schools' in this volume

18 Quoted in Habermas, J (1996) *Between Facts and Norms* Cambridge: Polity Press p490

TOMORROW'S WORLD

Citizenship and identity in the 21st century

Anthony Giddens
David Miller
Anne Phillips
Stuart Hall

1. Citizenship education in the global era

Anthony Giddens

This paper aims to move the discussion of citizenship forward by setting it against the background of the big changes going on in the world, and the impact they are having on our society. It is difficult to understand debates about citizenship or hope to educate people for it without grasping the nature of the transformations which are affecting not just the UK but all societies throughout the world.

Briefly, there are three big sets of changes. We are now well informed about them, but their consequences are far more difficult to puzzle through. The first is the implication of globalisation, which remains the focus of intense academic debate. What is it? Is it real? And is it different from the expansion of the western marketplace in different periods? My view is that that debate is more or less resolved; it *is* new, there are major changes going on in the world, bound up with the emergence of a new global electronic economy, and a much higher global level of integration than ever before. These changes have a series of consequences for institutions in a society like Britain.

What is important in this context is that they influence structures of governance. It is worth recalling the famous observation of the American sociologist Daniel Bell about the role of the nation in the global era: 'The nation-state becomes too small to solve the big problems but too big to solve the small ones'.[1] You have a movement of power upwards, but you also have strong downward pressure. That pressure is part of the condition under which you can hope to retrieve democracy, to restructure democratic association. The importance which the Labour party places upon community renewal is entirely consistent with what we know about how globalisation is reshaping our world.

The second series of changes is bound up with technology. When you think about technology you tend to think about Information Technology, and this is correct. IT is transforming the economy of western countries. There is no longer any doubt about this. It has altered the class structure; it is not globalisation itself but the increasing impact of IT which is the main cause of a radical shrinking of traditional blue-collar manufacturing jobs in western countries. You only have to recognise that most polities were structured round this class division until about 20 years ago to see how important technological change has been.

However, those in education also have to recognise that most technology is not confined to IT. We are in a new kind of society in our relation to science and innovation too. Science itself is becoming globalised. It has been calculated that there are more scientists working in the world today than have worked in the whole history of science before, and they are in communication with one another much more rapidly than was ever possible previously. Science simply invades our lives, much more directly than it ever did previously. When you consider the discussion about BSE in this country, it might be assumed that it is a one-off phenomenon – it is not. It is prototypical of a range of situations we will have to confront. The latest of these situations is genetically modified foods. These are political; they concern citizenship. We cannot any longer have a society in which we put technological change, or the impact of science, on one side, and expect the scientists to resume with their work. Part of the restructuring of citizenship has to be forming a sort of new dialogical relationship with science in which there are experts, but lay people, including children, will be called on to play a part.

Third is the impact of changes on our everyday life. You cannot get more fundamental than this. Very cursorily put, what is happening is that tradition and custom are still shaping our lives in western countries but much less than they used to do. We do not experience our lives as fate, as previous generations tended to do. The changing position of women across the world demonstrates how important this change has been and is now. A generation ago it was the fate of most women in western countries to have to settle for a life of domesticity, bringing up children and carrying out other duties. This is no longer is the case. What you make of your life as a woman is an open case, and of course the same now applies, in a refracted way, to the changing situation of men in a modern society.

These are truly global transformations; they are part of globalisation. They come back to the issue that Charles Clarke also raises: that of relationships and emotional life. Our emotional lives are wholly different from those of previous generations, not simply in a noxious way, though there are new anxieties that children and young women in particular feel. But there is a strong emancipatory side to this. This is what I have sometimes referred to as an emerging democratisation of the emotions. True democratisation of everyday life is just as important as formal democratisation in the political sphere, because it refers to the progress of equality between the sexes. This is not seen as just a legal principle or an economic phenomenon, but as an emotional part of what it is to be married, to be with another person, to be in a gay relationship, whatever it might be. So it is a really big package of change.

When you approach citizenship, four consequences can be identified. First, these changes have a major impact on sovereignty and the nature of national identity. These issues obviously arise in the sphere of citizenship, because it remains important to ask, 'citizen of what?' The nation-state is not disappearing or losing its power in the world, but it is being reshaped, especially in the West and especially in Europe. The European Union itself is becoming a kind of attempt to respond on a governmental level to globalisation. The outcome of this is that, especially in Europe, we are living in period of fuzzy sovereignty, in which nations are everywhere seeking to redefine their past, and recapture a new identity for the future. Living in such an era has its problems and some of these problems can be extremely acute: To some degree, it is possible to relate the conflict in Kosovo to the new-style relationship between territory boundaries in a cosmopolitan Europe. On the other hand, an era of fuzzy sovereignty offers us new possibilities. The peace process in Ireland, whether it is successful or not, would not have been possible without it. It is no longer a question of just being in or out of Northern Ireland. A citizen can be in Northern Ireland, connected to Ireland, connected to the UK, but also – crucially – connected to the European Union.

As far as education and citizenship are concerned, something clearly involved is tolerance of multiple identity. There is a new global battle in the world between cosmopolitanism and fundamentalism, whether a religious, ethnic or national fundamentalism. A cosmopolitan nation is one which enables every citizen to live comfortably with several identities, to be English, British, European, and perhaps even a citizen of a wider emerging world society. This is part of constructing a cosmopolitan nation: constructing, in the context of devolution and other changes that are responses to globalisation, an identity which is compatible with fuzzy sovereignty and the changing nature of international relations.

The second consequence is the impact of globalisation on political legitimacy and trust in politicians. W C Fields said, 'I never vote for anyone, I always vote against'.[2] Part of the problem in western countries is that a lot of people are not voting at all any more, and feel alienated from formal political processes. In most countries, according to surveys, people show less trust in politicians than they used to, and less trust in a range of other authority figures, including pillars of the establishment. These declining levels of trust are most marked among the younger generation, large proportions of whom simply do not vote, either in the US or in the majority of west European and other industrial countries. How do you address this legitimation deficit? It is a crucial part of reconstruction of citizenship and politics. The American political scientist Joe Nye uses excellent comparative evidence to show that people, even the younger generation, are not actually losing interest in politics.[3] They are, however, more cynical about orthodox democratic politics, about the role of orthodox parties, and about the pronouncements of orthodox political leaders. They are interested in questions that are not always on the political agenda, such as sexuality, lifestyle or ecological issues or animal rights. Or they simply think that politicians pretend to have power that they do not actually wield any more. They also respond to allegations of corruption, which are echoing in political circles round the world. This is partly because the nature of corruption changes in an open, globalised information society. Many ways of getting things done which were more or less accepted in the past are now seen as corrupt, especially by the younger generation. For example, leadership positions used to be fixed by old boy networks in this country until relatively recently. This is not acceptable any more, and politics must respond to this situation.

Third, the changing nature of the economy is fundamental. In a globalised, increasingly information dominated economy with a key role played by financial markets, it is impossible to maintain the same kinds of interventionism that left-of-centre governments practised before. Major new schisms also open up in the class structure. New forms of social exclusion appear as a result of the transformations in modern production systems. We have some very interesting findings on these issues, which are highly relevant to discussions of citizenship. Recent research on poverty in Germany shows that poverty and exclusion participate in the wider processes of the transformation of everyday life, as discussed earlier. Poverty is becoming less and less of a condition than it used to be, and is much more a kind of active phenomenon. The German research shows that people move in and out of poverty much more often than was previously thought and have a diversity of relationships to it. It is not a unitary phenomenon, but is actually highly differentiated. It is not a straightforward class phenomenon, and people have an active relationship to their life experiences, including their experiences of the welfare state. A basic part of Third Way politics is the thesis that the welfare state is not just something that protects people, but it has actually restructured people's lives, all the way through from the creation of pensions to the creation of benefit systems, and so on. This has multiple ramifications for anti-poverty policies and for citizenship.

Fourth, there have been fundamental changes in civil society. There is a rediscovery of civil society happening, not just in politics, where it goes back some fifteen years, but in everyday life. People are recovering forms of mutuality based upon community networks. An everyday discovery of what sociologists call 'social capital' is occurring around the world. This is resonant for discussions of citizenship because this is one of the areas where active citizenship is most pronounced. Voluntary associations, for example, are changing their nature. The old ones are declining, but there is a whole range of new ones, including self-help groups – many of them organised by younger people – changing and producing a more active civil society than has existed before. This is crucial, because it now has a new series of interconnections between business and government.

By focusing these dynamics on a discussion of citizenship itself, there are four points. The work of the Citizenship Advisory Group and of Bernard Crick in particular is extraordinarily important, and I fully support them in arguing for a 'highly educated citizen democracy'.[4] But this surely has to go against the backdrop of the other part of the programmes of political change that the Labour party and other parties are pushing for – which I think can be described as Second Wave Democratisation. This is how democratic countries respond to the legitimation deficit that I mentioned earlier. It involves many of the policies that the Labour party is already pursuing: devolution of power, constitutional reform, introduction of a Freedom of Information Act, however qualified it might be, and other changes relevant especially to the promotion of open information. You simply cannot run a country through traditional symbolism and backstage deals any more, and hope to retain political democracy. It is a major way of attempting to recover legitimacy for the political process. We need to reconstruct the nature of political institutions, but at the same time to bring onto the political agenda issues which have not previously been thought to be political. For example, we must find a way regularly to incorporate into the democratic process an appraisal – an ongoing appraisal, not just an ex *post facto* one – of the amazing impact which new forms of scientific information and innovation are having on our lives.

Second, citizenship operates now against the background of a new social contract. It has become pretty clear what the new social contract is. In a more open information society, where the state plays a reduced role and operates in conjunction with third sector groups, as everybody quite rightly says there is a new relationship between rights and responsibilities. I would like to sum this up by saying you try to operate by the principle of 'no rights without responsibilities'. However, you have to say that this must apply to everyone in society; it is no good having a principle of no rights without responsibilities that only applies to the poor, or to the excluded, or children, or other groups in society. It has to include business actors, pillars of the establishment and other powerful people. Education in citizenship may not make much impact unless it coincides with other structural reform, because there is an obvious problem with it, namely that the people who most need it are the people least likely to be interested in it.

We have to consider other structural issues too. One is developing a framework for regulation of corporate power. Corporate power is still a major aspect of the power structure of modern society, and the Government should be looking to set up regulatory frameworks, which allow the principle of no rights without responsibilities to apply to corporations as well as to individuals and other groups in wider society. This is not a Utopian view; however, it has to be done on an international as well as a national level.

Third, the Labour Government needs a more robust account of social justice, which is compatible with the changes now transforming the world. It is a problem, but also an opportunity for New Labour. This is the traditional old left critique of New Labour: not enough done about poverty, or about redistribution. But it cannot be done by using the old methods. For example, the welfare state has not been very good by and large in redistributional efforts. You have to look for new policies of social justice, which will reach the people in the impoverished parts of the country – this country has too much poverty compared to some other leading countries. The Labour party must address this in a systematic way, not just as a vote-getting mechanism, but as a true part of preserving its value inheritance. Policy-making has to be related to the new structures of poverty I have referred to. For example it might be better, rather than giving people money, to provide them with the opportunities to move from one role in life to another, or to allow them to accumulate savings at certain times of their lives.

Finally, education for citizenship has to be education of the critical spirit. Children live in a more reflexive society, and indoctrination has no place in a more open information society, whether you are poor or rich. Education in citizenship should above all be education of the critical spirit: a critical engagement with one's own position in society and an awareness of the wider forces to which all of us as individuals are responding.

Endnotes

1 Bell, D (1996) *The Cultural Contradictions of Capitalism* New York: Basic Books

2 Taylor, RL (1950) *WC Fields: His Follies and Fortunes* London: Penguin p228

3 Nye, JS, Zelikow, PD & King, DC (eds) (1997) *Why People don't Trust Government* Cambridge MA: Harvard University Press p253ff

4 Advisory Group on Citizenship (1998) *Education for Citizenship and the Teaching of Democracy in Schools* London: Qualifications and Curriculum Authority p9

2. Citizenship: what does it mean and why is it important?

David Miller

I do not intend in this essay to discuss directly the organisation of education for citizenship: that is a matter primarily for educationalists, and there is good work on that topic that I cannot hope to rival.[1] I *do* think, for reasons that will shortly become apparent, that the Labour Government's proposals to make citizenship education a formal part of the school curriculum are a step in the right direction. We cannot any longer assume that citizenship is something that people learn to do spontaneously, like eating and sleeping. What I hope to contribute instead are some thoughts about what it means to be a citizen, and about why even among people who are favourably disposed towards strengthening citizenship there is a great deal of confusion as to what this entails in practice. I shall also underline some of the difficulties involved in being a citizen in a world where political identities are steadily becoming more complex and fragmented.

Citizenship – except in the formal passport-holding sense – is not a widely understood idea in Britain. People do not have a clear idea of what it means to be a citizen, as opposed to being one of her Majesty's subjects. (Indeed even passports have only referred to their holders as *citizens* rather than *subjects* since, appropriately, their jackets have turned from blue to red.) Citizenship is not a concept that has played a central role in our political tradition, in contrast for example to France, where the revolutionary tradition of 1789 has made the idea of French citizenship a touchstone for debate ever since. We are still inclined to see citizenship as slightly foreign and slightly unsettling – the citizen is a busybody who goes around disturbing the easy-going, tolerant quality of life in Britain. Let me give two examples from a misspent youth watching low-brow television. When the BBC wanted to make a sitcom about revolutionary youth in the 1970s, it called it Citizen Smith. Implicit message: the citizen is an impractical idealist who goes around trying to mobilise a population which has no intention at all of being mobilised. Second example: when the Carry On Team decided to do the French Revolution, the three traits you notice about the French is that they're homicidal, very silly, and always address one another as Citizen

This or That. Implicit message: the citizen is not only an impractical idealist, but also foreign and generally laughable.

Some of these doubts and uncertainties about citizenship come through in more academic studies of what the general public thinks it means to be a citizen, or a good citizen. A study a few years back using focus groups found that for British people citizenship was primarily understood in terms of a bundle of rights and obligations.[2] In other words, as a citizen, you have a set of rights, including the right to legal protection and the right to vote, but most especially social rights, rights to a minimum standard of living, to education, to medical care and so forth. In return you have certain obligations, for instance to keep the law, and to contribute through tax or social insurance to the cost of securing those rights. So for the majority of people in these groups, to be a good citizen was to be a law-abiding member of the community, and to engage in an essentially private set of activities such as holding a responsible job and raising a family. The idea that citizenship should also involve political or communal participation was a minority view. It was not that people positively disapproved of the person who is active in local politics or the parent-teacher association, but, instead, they recognised a division of labour so that not everyone need be an activist in order to be a good citizen.

Three models of citizenship can be identified in recent political debate.[3] Although these are not mutually exclusive in practice, they rest upon different underlying philosophies – different ways of understanding the value of being a citizen. The first, liberal model is the one that the focus groups described above were mainly using – citizenship understood as a set of rights and obligations that gives every citizen an equal status in the political community. Following TH Marshall, we can interpret the development of democratic societies as involving a progressive extension of the rights of citizenship, with civil rights coming first, political rights next and social rights last.[4] Liberal citizenship has been largely but not fully achieved in these societies: its continuing importance as a critical concept is to provide a point of leverage, particularly when social policy is being discussed. We want to make sure that there are no second class citizens, so we have to try to ensure that education, medical care and the other rights of citizenship are available to everyone on an equal basis. However, the limitation of this model of citizenship is that the citizen herself remains relatively passive, her active role being simply that of defending her rights by voting in periodic elections.

The second model develops the first in one direction by seeing the citizen as a consumer of public services who therefore has consumers' rights. This is the citizen as found in the Citizens' Charters of the early 1990s. The citizen is entitled to expect a certain standard of service or provision, and is empowered to seek compensation or redress if the service is not satisfactory. This gives citizenship a more active flavour, but it remains a somewhat individualistic understanding of the idea. For instance, if the Railway Operator fails to make the trains run on time, then I as an individual am entitled to redress by getting some part of my money back. I may join forces with some other disgruntled travellers, but that is incidental. There is no sense here that citizenship is an essentially communal activity. Nor does it have a democratic character: the Charter is not drawn up by the citizens themselves, but handed down from on high by politicians and civil servants. There is nothing wrong with the idea of a Citizens' Charter – it is obviously important to have a means whereby recipients can monitor the quality of public services. Yet citizenship understood solely in terms of having rights of redress against service providers is a narrow and impoverished version of that concept.

Model three, the minority view among the general public, is that the citizen is not only a rights-holder and a claimant, but someone who is actively involved in shaping the way that his or her community functions. We could distinguish here between political involvement in the narrow sense, such as being involved in political campaigning or serving on a city or parish council, and public activity that need not have a political character such as helping to refurbish the village hall or being an active member of the local conservation group. Both of these are examples of active citizenship. Indeed, citizenship on this model must involve more than just activism per se; it must also involve a sense of public responsibility, a sense that what you are doing is for the good of the public as a whole, not merely one sectional interest. So, for instance, the lobbyist who acts on behalf of a particular industry is obviously politically active but is not in this respect acting as a citizen. Clearly, model three citizenship is appealing in certain ways – even if it does conjure up in some minds Robert Lindsay as Citizen Smith or Kenneth Williams as Citizen Camembert. However, it is also considerably more demanding, both in terms of time and in terms of the ethical demands it makes upon the individual, than models one and two. We may wonder whether many people really want to, or are able to function as citizens in this sense.

The chief appeal of model three is perhaps that it offers us the image of a democratic society, a society in which ordinary people are heavily involved in deciding issues and achieving goals, not just voting for governments and then letting governments make decisions for them. If we are going to move in that direction, then we have to face up to the issue of political conflict and disagreement, the fact that people really do have conflicting interests and ideals. If we are going to rely on active citizenship to decide issues, then citizens have to be prepared to see beyond their own interests and commitments and take a wider, more impartial view. At present, much political activity takes the form of one-sided commitment to particular causes; people are engaged in campaigning for the environment, or in protecting jobs in a particular industry threatened with decline. There is nothing wrong in this, but it does depend on some higher authority being willing to act as an adjudicator, rather than the people themselves. So when a new by-pass is mooted, we are likely to have a lobby of local people fed up with congested roads confronting a protest movement of ecological activists. The issue is resolved by a public enquiry at the end of which some wise and impartial inspector delivers a verdict. If issues such as this were to be resolved democratically, it would require large numbers of citizens to take a relatively detached view, weighing the benefit to the local town of having the by-pass against the cost to the environment of building it. This is a demanding condition, because empirically it seems to be the case that the people most likely to be politically involved and active are those who are not detached at all, but have a particular moral commitment or particular interest to motivate them.

This leads to the question of political identity and how citizenship is connected to it. To be a citizen in my third sense, you have to identify with the broader political community within which citizen activity is going to take place. It is this identification that gives you a sense of responsibility for the whole, and not merely the particular subgroup you belong to, whether this is an ethnic group, or a group of like-minded activists. The very idea of citizenship, as its etymology suggests, first appeared in cities – by our standards small cities, such as classical

Athens or renaissance Florence. These city-states cultivated intense feelings of loyalty among their citizens (who were of course male, as Anne Phillips' chapter reminds us) – feelings strong enough to allow factional and sectional divisions to be overcome. In this sense, citizens were finally willing to put the good of the city above their personal concerns. As city-states ceased to be viable as independent political communities, nation-states increasingly took their place. Nations were 'imagined communities', in Benedict Anderson's evocative phrase.[5] Their members could not know one another personally, and so their sense of common identity depended on mass media of communication to convey to each member the character of the community to which he or she belonged. Yet this collective imagining was successful insofar as nations produced a strong sense of identity and commitment among their members, demonstrated especially in willingness to fight and die on the nation's behalf. Although active citizenship in nation-states has typically been the preserve of the few, the resources for citizenship, in the sense of a shared identity that could motivate people to behave as responsible citizens, have always been present.

The problem we face today is that political identities are tending to fragment. They are fragmenting first because the shape of the political community itself is becoming more complex. We have to think in terms now not just of British politics but also of Scottish, Welsh and Irish politics, and then of course of European politics. One result is that we may begin to have multi-layered political identities among which no one level is clearly dominant and we have then to ask how our notions of citizenship should change to accommodate this. Are we to be citizens of just one state, or of several interlocked political communities? Additionally, political identities are also fragmenting because of the rise within each political community of ethnic and other subcultures that confer on their members a strong sense of separation and distinctness. Cultural differences are of course not in themselves new, but what is perhaps new is the idea that your cultural identity may constitute your primary political identity. For instance, if you are an animal rights campaigner, or a gay activist, or a religious fundamentalist, then this matters more to you politically than, say, your responsibilities as a British citizen.

So we are caught in something of a dilemma. On the one hand there are good reasons, in terms of general democratic values, for moving towards a more active model of citizenship, going beyond model one and model two in the direction of model three. On the other hand, we seem increasingly to lack the secure political identities that could underpin that model. We do not have a strong, overriding sense of ourselves as British that would give us the motivation to behave as responsible citizens in the way I have described.

My own view concerning this matter is controversial. We cannot have active citizenship in the modern world, without inclusive national identities to support it. Consequently, it is important to find ways in which existing national identities can accommodate the various kinds of cultural divisions that exist in contemporary societies.[6] This means in part that we have to become more self-conscious about national identity; we have to abandon the lazy idea that being British and being English are pretty much the same, for instance, or more crudely still that to be British you have to be a WASP. We have to get to grips with the phenomenon of 'nested' national identities, whereby people can identify equally strongly with a larger nation-state and with a smaller national community inside it, as for instance Catalans in Spain or Scots in Britain are increasingly doing. We have to learn to distinguish what is really part of national political culture (and which, therefore, we are justified in promoting among all groups of citizens) and what is simply the culture of a particular ethnic, religious or regional group (and which, therefore, should generally be left for groups to develop spontaneously according to their own beliefs and values). So our understanding of national identity must be a flexible one. But at the same time, we must recognise that we cannot teach people to be citizens without teaching them to be members of a national community. Citizenship is not simply a matter of personal morality, of learning not to steal or to beat people up in the street. Nor is it simply a matter of political effectiveness, of knowing which buttons to press if you want to get a government grant or to claim a benefit. If you are going to be an active and responsible citizen, involved in doing things on behalf of the community as a whole, then you must have an understanding of what that community stands for. And that in turn means having a sense of yourself as a member of a historic community in whose positive achievements you can justifiably take pride, and of whose shortcomings you should feel ashamed.

Today, it is frequently argued – this argument was put to me on several occasions on a recent visit to Germany – that nation-states have little scope for deciding issues independently from one another, so that viable forms of citizenship must now occur in larger units. In particular, it's claimed that Europe itself might come to serve as a source of identity and citizenship that overrides existing national allegiances. This certainly is the hope of some European leaders today. But is it a realistic hope, and should we be supporting moves in this direction?

Currently, it is fairly clear that for people across Europe, the nation remains their primary focus of political identity and allegiance. If asked who they are willing to fight to defend, or who they are willing to support by paying taxes, the answer given by people in each country, is their fellow-nationals.[7] Attitudes to the general idea of European unity are broadly positive – though views about the European Union as an institution are more divided, with majorities in some countries saying that on balance they would be better out than in. However, Europe does not command loyalty in the ways that nation-states do. A united Europe is seen as a useful arrangement that provides benefits like freer travel and greater access to jobs and economic markets, but it does not generate a sense of emotional identification.

Even if Europe cannot yet provide the sense of identity that nations can, does it not at least provide a transnational form of citizenship that might be the precursor of transnational citizenship in other parts of the world? Certainly, European citizenship exists in a legal sense. But what does this mean in practice?[8] European citizens enjoy some rights that are not available to outsiders, for example the rights to travel freely across borders within Europe, and to work and study in other European countries. They also have the right to challenge national legislation or policy by bringing a case before the European Court of Justice. This latter right has had some significance in forcing national governments to come into line with European practice in some areas. But its reach should not be exaggerated. The European Court has been careful to construe its remit quite narrowly so as not to challenge the right of member states to pursue different policies in areas such as health, education and industrial relations according to national traditions and preferences.

If we look at European citizenship from a political perspective, it is clear that it does not yet exist in any substantive sense. Knowledge of and interest in the doings of the European parliament and the other institutions of the Union are minimal, as the alarmingly low turnout in the 1999 elections to the European parliament has reminded us. Moreover, European elections are fought very largely by national parties on national issues. Politically speaking, people continue overwhelmingly to think and act as members of national electorates. As for social citizenship, rights to health, education, social security, pensions and so forth remain under the control of national governments, subject only to such common standards as are imposed by the European treaties and enforced by the Court of Justice. As I pointed out a moment ago, this still leaves room for considerable variation in how these rights are defined. It would be hard to claim that European social citizenship exists in any concrete sense.

If this is a correct assessment of the current situation, what are the prospects of the European Union changing in such a way that we might witness the development of a European-wide practice of democratic citizenship? One serious obstacle to this, as Tony Judt has emphasised in his book *A Grand Illusion*, is the continuing existence of language divisions among the peoples of Europe.[9] Although negotiations among political elites are increasingly carried out using English as a common language (French resistance to this practice seems finally to be crumbling), if we are looking towards a form of democratic politics in which the public at large are involved in political debate, we must recognise that such debate will necessarily be carried out in the vernacular language of each community. We cannot expect the ordinary citizens of Italy, Denmark or Greece to conduct their political discussions using English, or any other second language for that matter. So these debates will remain opaque to those who speak a different language. Instead of a European public opinion, which might form the basis of a European-wide form of democracy, the best we can hope for are separate bodies of public opinion that could then be fed into elite negotiations at European level. There seems to be a simple trade-off here: the wider the scope of citizenship is drawn, and the more publics it has therefore to embrace, the weaker its democratic credentials become.

If we want people to understand citizenship better and have a stronger sense of their own identity as citizens, we should focus primarily on citizenship at the national level. If that can be achieved – and I have been stressing the difficulties as well as the importance of the task – people who are used to acting as citizens in national arenas will be better prepared to act responsibly outside them as well. But to try to jump from the present situation, where active citizenship is still a minority concern, to a transformation of political identities that will make us all into active European citizens in one go, seems to me a leap too far.

Finally, what does all of this entail for citizenship education? If we are going to educate our children to become citizens, then we need to decide, obviously enough, what it means to be a citizen. Is it a matter of being a law-abiding member of the community, of having an essentially moral grasp of right and wrong? Or is it a matter of knowing what the state can do for you, how to ensure that you get what you are entitled to from public agencies? I have suggested that, important though these two aspects of citizenship are, they are not sufficient. To be a citizen in the fullest sense you must in some way be actively involved in shaping the way that your community develops, whether this is through political activity in the strict sense or through public involvement of a non-political kind. This also seems to be the view of the Crick report on *Education for Citizenship*. But in that case we also need to decide what our future citizens are going to be citizens *of*: it is impossible to disentangle citizenship from the issue of nationality, of the nature and boundaries of the political community to which someone belongs. Unfortunately, as I have indicated, it is no longer possible – certainly not in Britain – to say that we belong to just one such political community. Depending on who we are and where we live, we may find that our political identity is split between two or three different levels. So citizenship education will have to come to terms with this fact. One of its tasks will be to explain how the different levels of identity have emerged historically, and how they are now related – what it now means to be Scottish in Britain or British in Europe. These are hard concepts to grasp; most people, I suspect, find single-level identities easier to deal with.[10] But the task cannot be ducked. Although I have cautioned against leaping straight to European citizenship as the primary focus, it is not my intention to recommend a narrow, insular nationalism in its place. National identity matters, and as we continue to debate the meaning of Britishness at the turn of the century, we should not hesitate to pass down our best understanding of this idea to the rising generation through the education system. But I also believe that Britishness itself will increasingly become a hyphenated identity, and that, too, is something that needs to be passed on when we teach our children about citizenship.

Endnotes

1 There is also good work by political philosophers on the meaning of education for citizenship. See especially Gutmann, A (1986) *Democratic Education* Princeton, NJ: Princeton University Press, and Callan, E (1997) *Creating Citizens: Political Education and Liberal Democracy* Oxford: Clarendon Press

2 Conover, PJ, Crewe, IM and Searing, DD (1991) 'The Nature of Citizenship in the United States and Great Britain: Empirical Comments on Theoretical Themes' *Journal of Politics* 53

3 I draw here on my analysis of citizenship in (1995) 'Citizenship and Pluralism' *Political Studies* 43

4 Marshall, TH in Bottomore, T(ed) (1992) *Citizenship and Social Class* London: Pluto Press (originally published 1950). For discussion of some of the difficulties with Marshall's sequence of citizenship rights, see Rees, A 'TH Marshall and the progress of citizenship' in Bulmer, M and Rees, AM (eds) (1996) *Citizenship Today: The Contemporary Relevance of TH Marshall* London: UCL Press

5 Anderson, B (1991) *Imagined Communities* (rev edn) London: Verso

6 I have explored these questions in greater depth in Miller, D (1995) *On Nationality* Oxford: Clarendon Press

7 For evidence that bears this out, see Ashford, S and Timms, N (1992) *What Europe Thinks: A Study of Western European Values* Aldershot: Dartmouth and Hewstone, M (1986) *Understanding Attitudes to the European Community* Cambridge: Cambridge University Press

8 For a thorough analysis, see Meehan, E (1993) *Citizenship and the European Community* London: Sage

9 Judt, T (1997) *A Grand Illusion: An Essay on Europe* London: Penguin

10 It is also difficult to get to grips with political systems that work in unfamiliar ways. When I was trying to explain the European election results to my two sons, ages 8 and 10, their first (and only) question was 'But who has won?' If you are used to a electoral system whose function is to eject one government and install another, it is difficult to understand a parliament in which clear winners and losers never emerge

3. Second class citizenship

Anne Phillips

One of the problems of citizenship is that it divides people into those who belong and those who do not. It promises an equality of treatment to all who qualify as citizens, but may in the process relieve us of moral responsibilities to those who remain outside. This problem looms large in contemporary discussions of European citizenship (the fears of 'fortress Europe'), and is sharply exemplified by current policies on the treatment of refugees. But there is a further problem that surfaces even within the recognized citizen community; some of those who share in the official rights and responsibilities of citizenship may still feel themselves treated as less than full members. They may feel, that is, that they are only 'second-class citizens'.

Women have often used the phrase 'second-class citizenship' to capture a perception that being female put them in a lesser category than being male, that it makes them poorer, less powerful, less likely to be taken seriously, or, at best, positions them as an interesting addition to discourses that continue to be framed and defined by men. The historical background to this is that women did *not* have the same rights and responsibilities as men. Men had the right to vote when women did not; men had a duty to serve on juries when women were exempted; men were conscripted to serve in the armed forces when women were not. As late as the 1960s, the US Supreme Court judged that it was acceptable for a state to require men to serve on juries while leaving it up to the women to volunteer (since few of us think of volunteering for jury service, this usually generated all-male juries). This practice was justified by reference to women's 'special' responsibilities to family and home. At this point in history – not so very long ago – the rights and responsibilities of citizenship were still seen as firmly gendered; and while this gendering of citizenship was usually presented as a matter of different rather than unequal treatment, many women felt they were being treated as lesser than men.

The more typical experience today is not distinctive schedules of rights and responsibilities, tailored to what are supposed to be quintessentially male and female roles. There is, however, a very different working out of our supposedly equal rights, and a continuing perception of women as the oddities or exceptions in most of the contexts where decisions are taken about our collective lives. Women then find themselves marked by their sex in a way that is less common to men. The parallel experience for many black people – in this case, particularly for black men – is even starker. When black people are persistently stopped for police questioning because they have wandered too close to the scene of a crime or are driving a car thought too expensive to be legitimately their own, they are not just being treated as outside the norm but as the objects of active suspicion. Citizenship is supposed to confer an equal status on all citizens, regardless of sex, race, ethnicity, or religion, regardless of whether one is rich or poor. But it does not, as we know, do this. One of the key questions in any education for citizenship is what else has to change in order for that ideal of citizenship to become more real.

In much earlier discussion, it was thought that the answer to that question lay in the extension of the social rights of citizenship. We had civil rights (equal rights to freedoms of speech and religion, equal rights to due process of law). We had political rights (equal rights to vote and participate in the exercise of political power). But full membership of the citizen community was thought to depend also on social rights (to education, for example, welfare, employment) that would, in TH Marshall's words, enable each of us 'to live the life of a civilised being according to the standards prevailing in the society'.[1] Marshall notoriously failed to grasp the nettle of sexual equality in his understanding of those social rights, and as feminist theorists have noted, continued to operate with an image of man as breadwinner, woman as dependant.[2] The general thesis he laid out, nonetheless, has provided the inspiration for an understanding of citizenship as premised on certain social and economic conditions. In this understanding, citizenship implies not just formal but some substantive equality. It thrives in conditions where all have access to what is necessary to a decent life; it is severely disrupted by what today we term social exclusion.

I shall return to that earlier way of answering the questions of citizenship, for one of the points I want to make is that we have wandered too far from the social rights of citizenship, come to think of citizenship too exclusively as a political, legal, or cultural matter, and stopped thinking seriously enough about the economic conditions for treating citizens as equals. Part of this shift is, in my view, a retreat, a backing away from what post-war theorists of citizenship rightly regarded as a crucial part of the picture. But there has been a positive side to that process as well, for it has opened up much unfinished business around the political and civil rights of citizenship, and alerted us to a number of problems that are often theorised under the heading of equality and difference.

In numerical terms, those of us who are female or come from a minority racial or ethnic group make up the majority of citizens, yet this numerical majority is still constituted as the oddities, the exceptions, in many ways the outsiders. It has often been noted that people talk of ethnicity, for example, as if it were something attached only to people who are in a minority, so that minority groups become defined by their ethnicity while the ethnicity of majority groups remains invisible. Women, I have already suggested, are marked by their sex in a way that men are not: we talk of 'women's issues'; we count the number of women in politics; we notice when someone in a position of influence is a woman; but we are much less likely to think about maleness as a defining characteristic. To give just one of many illustrations, students will typically learn about the struggle for male suffrage in a course on British history; they will learn about the struggle for female suffrage – if at all – in courses on feminist politics.

There is a taken-for-grantedness about the current dispensation of power and influence that is deeply troubling, and one of the strategic problems this poses to groups trying to challenge it is whether to rally around the recognition of difference. If normality has been defined as male, white, heterosexual, Church of England, one obvious way to do battle against that misleading and homogenising perception is to make the differences more visible: to emphasise just how many citizens there are who do not fit the image of the 'typical' citizen; to stress their multiplicity and variation; to insist on an educational curriculum that reflects this diversity; to take issue with the notion that equality depends on sameness. But part of the problem of second-class citizenship is that those outside the norm get defined by their differences in ways that those inside it do not, that women are gendered when men are not; that black people are racialised when white people are not; that Bangladeshis are seen as 'ethnic' when 'white European' is just an empty residual category. Rallying around difference may not be the best way to tackle this problem. It could just confirm the image of the standard citizen, but now surrounded by a more visible penumbra of 'others' characterised primarily by their difference.

Part of what is at stake here are alternative ways of conceiving of citizen equality. From what we might call the anti-discrimination perspective, the key ideal is that all citizens, regardless of their differences, ought to be treated the same. There should not be one law for the rich, another for the poor, there should not be one set of rights for women, another set for men, there should not be one kind of treatment meted out to white citizens and another kind to black. This is an ideal that clearly has a lot going for it. It would not, for example, allow for that gendering of citizen rights and responsibilities I have mentioned as part of the background against which women came to feel themselves second class citizens; it would not allow for the harassment of black citizens because of the colour of their skin. But there are important reservations about this as the main way of conceiving of citizen equality, one being that the anti-discrimination paradigm can encourage a pretence that the differences do not matter (they should not matter therefore we will not let them matter). This can end up as an egalitarian gloss that leaves us with the old status quo. Sometimes we have to attach weight to differences in order to deal with the inequalities attached to them, and simply saying we should treat all citizens as equals does not provide enough of a way forward.

Consider the serious under-representation of women and ethnic minority groups in British political life. It is hard to conceive of a solution to this that does not involve some form of affirmative action, some deliberate action by political parties – as in the Labour Party's use of all-women short lists to select candidates for the last general election, or the decision to 'twin' constituencies for elections to the Scottish Parliament so as to ensure a better balance between women and men. It is difficult, that is, to think of ways of addressing the problem of under-representation that do not involve some intervention in the 'natural' order of things, some positive action that makes the sex, and by the same token, the ethnicity, of the candidates a matter of conscious concern.[3] It is also difficult to conceive of a solution to racism in the police force that does not involve significantly raising the proportion of ethnic minority police officers. The recent Government endorsement of targets for recruitment represents an important step in that direction. If we were to adopt the simpler anti-discrimination paradigm that says we should ignore differences of sex, race, or ethnicity in the selection of candidates for the police force or political office, we would not be able to endorse such initiatives. All of them depend on taking difference more, rather than less seriously, and actively promoting a different distribution of jobs or influence or power.

There is a further criticism often raised against the anti-discrimination perspective, which is that it does not sufficiently question the way the norms have been set. It is sometimes read as promising to treat women as if they are as good as any man, promising to treat Jews and Muslims as if they are the same as any Christian, promising to look beyond the accidents of skin colour to the essential humanity beneath. When read in this way, it seems to reinforce the notion that these peculiarities really are peculiar. If people are obliged to discount aspects of themselves in order to qualify for equal treatment, they may come to feel this as a rather grudging kind of acceptance. They will be accepted into the fold, but only on condition that they highlight their similarities, cover over their differences, make themselves more like those who are already full citizens in order to be welcomed as their equal.

Both these problems set serious limits to the purer anti-discrimination model. I do not subscribe to the idea that equality between citizens is best achieved through disregarding or ignoring our differences; we have evidence enough to suggest that this is an inadequate solution. But if part of what characterises existing inequalities in citizenship is that certain categories of citizen are regarded as normal, while others are defined through their difference, then stressing the differences could reinforce the tendency to characterise the more marginal (and never the others) precisely by their differences. We need, it seems, to recognise and validate difference, but we need also to challenge the definition of peoples by their 'difference'. Where do we go from here?

Though this may seem an insoluble dilemma, it is better regarded as a healthy reminder of some of the issues to be addressed in thinking about an education for citizenship that is about women as well as men, ethnic minorities as well as ethnic majorities. If we do not 'name' women as distinct from men, we are likely to perpetuate an unthinking association of citizens with men. If we do not 'name' cultural, religious, or ethnic difference, we are likely to perpetuate a misleading image of national identity as coinciding with majority groups. Ignoring difference makes certain groups of citizens less visible. But there is clearly a risk on the other side of making women stand in for everything to do with gender (so that men have no gender while women have nothing else); and a risk of exoticising ethnic minorities as if their ethnicity captures everything about them. If difference is attached only to the marginal, their citizenship is still second class. Part of the way forward must be to recognise that *all* of us are different in many different ways, and that being 'different' is itself the norm.

This is one issue that needs to be addressed in thinking about education and citizenship. The other issue is that the new emphasis on what it means to recognise and validate differences between citizens threatens to close off some of the earlier questions about the social and economic conditions for equal citizenship. In the older paradigm (derived very much from worries about class inequalities), it was widely recognised that the enjoyment of citizen rights is affected by economic conditions: that it is harder for the poor than the rich to secure redress through the law courts; that it is easier for the well-educated and articulate to influence the course of a public enquiry; that middle class citizens have been able to make more of their equal right to participate in politics than citizens from the working class. Sometimes people then looked to a variety of political mechanisms that could strengthen the rights and participation of the poor, but mostly it was assumed that the answers were economic. If economic inequalities were blocking the equal exercise of citizenship, the solution was to reduce the range. Redistributive taxation would close the gap between the richest and the poorest, while the welfare system would make health care and education equally available to all. The life-experiences of rich and poor would come closer together, and the ideals of citizenship would become more real.

Though only a tiny minority envisaged full equalisation, there was certainly an expectation of convergence. Today, by contrast, we are encouraged to dismiss convergence as 'levelling down' or 'the politics of envy', to focus our attention on opportunities rather than outcome, to tackle poverty, perhaps, but not worry unduly about inequality. One of the ironies here is that new thinking on difference could help legitimate this process, for as we become more conscious of the dangers of assimilationism, we may inadvertently reinforce the retreat from economic equality.

As the analysis of inequality has broadened out from a purely class understanding to address further inequalities associated with gender, ethnicity or race, it has made some aspects of the convergence model more suspect. We clearly cannot make equality of citizenship depend on half the population undergoing a sex change; we cannot make it depend on mass programmes of racial intermarriage that eliminate differences in skin colour; we cannot (or, at least, should not) make it conditional on convergence between the diverse cultural practices or religious beliefs that exist within the citizen body. People are, quite rightly, suspicious of the assimilationism that makes equality depend on sameness, or regards people as equals only when they become like one another in every conceivable way. But it sometimes seems that this (entirely legitimate) critique of assimilationism spills over into a lack of interest in any kind of economic convergence. It is as if recognising that not all equalities depend on citizens becoming more alike prevents us noticing those that still do.

And yet some, at least, of the inequalities in citizenship continue to revolve around stark inequalities in income or housing or education or jobs. Some, at least of the inequalities can only be dealt with through processes of convergence. Indeed, the 'second-class citizenship' of women or members of ethnic minority groups is still very much bound up with economic indicators and it would be a sad irony if the process of thinking through new issues of difference contributed to an amnesia on these concerns. The task, in other words, is to knit these different discourses together, to remind ourselves that there are certain material conditions without which equality of citizenship cannot thrive, while building into this a more nuanced understanding of the relationship between equality and difference.

Endnotes

1 Marshall, TH (1950) *Citizenship and Social Class* Cambridge: Cambridge University Press

2 See, for example, the discussion in Lister, R (1997) *Feminist Perspectives* London: Macmillan

3 For a fuller development of this argument, see Phillips, A (1995) *The Politics of Presence* Oxford: Oxford University Press

4. Multicultural citizens, monocultural citizenship?

Stuart Hall

This paper aims to address a continuing theme on the question of citizenship, and citizenship education, in the context of what has sometimes been too self-congratulatorily called 'the irresistible rise of multicultural Britain'.

These issues are very similar to some of the arguments which Anne Phillips also highlights. I will try both to draw from and relate to some of the points which she has made. To return to something very fundamental, the western concepts of citizenship do depend, in a central way, on the capacity of the government or state to guarantee rights, to protect equally, and consequently to demand obligations from those who dwell within the reach of its authority, and owe allegiance to it. Its universality, which is a central feature of it, has been underpinned by this overlap between political authority and territorial sovereignty.

Anthony Giddens seems to assert that, although the disappearance of the nation-state is not on the agenda, it has been severely restricted in its reach by political developments, which are both above and below the level of the nation. From a wider perspective, this takes the form of globalisation. However, the concept of globalisation in some ways seriously misrepresents it. This is because it tends to focus our minds on what is happening above the level of the nation-state, and defers focus on the crucial developments that occur on the level below that. However, both above and below, and indeed the authority and allegiance to the nation-state itself, have all been transformed and redistributed by the forms of globalisation which have become so dominating. This has particularly been the case in the last three to four decades.

The question of multiculturalism and of Britain as a multiethnic society does suggest that to some degree questions of citizenship are undermined, not simply by the relative weakening of the reach of the nation-state as a political entity, but also by the growth of cultural diversity. This aspect comes to the fore when we ask the question: 'What is the status of citizenship in a society whose self-understanding is that it is increasingly multicultural and multiethnic?' What is it about cultural diversity that threatens to weaken some of the conceptions of citizenship,which we have taken for granted?

This may be because the nation-state is both a political entity and what I would call a focus for identification, an imagined community. As well as organising our lives as citizens together through political and legal authority, it is an entity that produces a measure of effective identification, and a sense of belonging. In spite of the ways in which the nation-state has been thought of in classic orthodox liberal theory, it does have cultural as well as political, legal and economic foundations. The classic theory of the nation-state in liberal orthodoxy would suggest that the constitutional state must deal with the formal equality and status of individuals, citizens conceived as abstract individuals. Its universality depends on its capacity to hold at bay, or indeed to abolish to the sphere of private life, all those cultural particularities which threaten to undermine its universality. This has been a very important element in the early rise of the liberal constitutional state. Such a conception of the state is still very powerfully grounded, for example, in the United States. This is one of the reasons why many believe that affirmative action seems to entrammel the state in exactly those cultural particularities which it ought to abstain from. The idea is that it is acceptable to transfer cultural diversity into the sphere of the domestic and the private. You can listen to as large and as loud a transistor set in the privacy of your own house as you like, and listen to anything on it, provided you do not disturb the neighbours. The moment you intrude into the public sphere, the state should not make a difference depending on whether you are male or female, black or white, or what ethnic group or religious faith you belong to.

Liberal societies claim to adhere to this kind of narrative, but it has never been true, and is much less true now than it has ever been before. The nation-state, in so far as it is able to mobilise a sense of identity and belonging on the part of the people, has always been deeply mired in particular cultural meanings. The only difference is that the cultural meanings are assumed to be very widely shared. They are part of what we might call the British way of life, or English common sense, or reasonableness, and all those other wonderfully shared things which underpin the legal system, the operation of the common law and so on. How many readers have recently travelled on the top of a Clapham omnibus? It is no longer a repository of good, stout English common sense. You are most likely to find no grown men on it – they are in the cars outside trying to get past; it is full of women, small children and geriatrics. The notion that the sense of what goes and does not go in this society is shared across the seats of this vehicle of transportation is completely ludicrous. It does not correspond to our everyday experience of the fact that you have to work quite hard to construct the reasonable Englishman's view of what should be right or wrong in a whole range of very important personal and social relationships.

The liberal state, in spite of its account of itself, has always been deeply lodged in culture. It has its own ethnicity, but there are two great effects of that. On the one hand, that cultural life has been very widely shared, creating a kind of homogeneity over a long period of time, so it is difficult to see how this homogeneity has been constructed, and to locate the gaps. It has also been in a position to declare its particularity as universal. It says, 'the way we do things is how folks should do things'. That is why, when people do not do things in that way, they are marked as different. Differences are not seen as being deeply lodged inside the nation-state itself.

Political theorists are not dealing with this issue very extensively and certainly not as extensively in this country as they are dealing with it elsewhere. Liberal theory no longer describes the real world in which we live. There are four ways in which this has an impact on the question of citizenship.

First, the result of globalisation has broken the exclusive link between geography, sovereignty and political power – it no longer has the exclusive reach that it had in previous periods. Citizens are at risk in a much wider network of relations, both beyond and below the reach of the nation-state. Although the nation-state remains a very important factor in defining rights and responsibilities, and in adjudicating our relations as citizens to one another, it is no longer in any sense the only critical arena in which those rights are exclusively defined.

Second, the much intensified global exchanges between countries, societies and cultures has been going on for a long time, through world trade, colonisation, exploration and the expansion of the West. However, the mass migrations of recent decades, which are either forced or so-called 'free', have mixed up populations and cultures. These exist not only at the colonial periphery where they have always been mixed up, but in the metropolitan centres themselves. This has intensified the plurality or diversification of the so-called cultures of the citizens themselves. As a consequence, the assumed homogeneity of a common British way of life, which can be taken as forming the cultural or value background against which political and legal decisions can be taken with respect to the citizens, no longer has the uninspected status of the natural order of things. In other words, these irrevocable differences have arrived in a world which we have tried to live in and experience relatively homogeneously. In such a world, we did not need to worry too much about the differences between one group and another.

This may be attributable to the fact of us turning up at the end of the imperial period; just when you thought you had got rid of us, we moseyed on home in a couple of banana boats to see whether the stories you had been telling us for four hundred years were true. It is a tragic paradox that we showed up just at the wrong moment. You were hauling down the flag as we turned up at Tilbury – a kind of disjuncture of these two worlds colliding with one another.

This suggests that this cultural diversity belongs only to a relatively small area of society, to the cities and the places of high migratory settlement. The term 'multicultural', however, has to include the enormous pluralisation of forms of life amongst the majority populations themselves. Technological, social, economic, political and moral changes have created far more internally diversified and plural cultures for the majority. The loss of empire, coupled with the relative economic decline and the political disaggregation of the United Kingdom, further eroded that structure of instabilities, inequalities, which we used to call The British Way of Life. The growth of supranational power draws power and identification away from the centre. At the same time it intensifies the sense of local differences, which are not the opposite of but deeply enmeshed with this process of globalisation. The local is as reorganised by the global as the international and intra-state relations are, intensifying the revival of a certain localism, or ethnic particularism. This underpins for example the movement towards devolution.

The fourth area I would identify is a breakdown of the neat division which was implicit in my point on the conceptions of the state in relation to cultural difference in the past: the breakdown of the so-called public and private divide. This notion is that there is a neat and well-established distinction between the private and public, where you can say, 'Go and practise your religion, your cultural differences, your ethnic oddities and so on behind closed curtains. Once you come into the public sphere you have to obey a different regime.' This is completely undermined by the intrusion of the public into the private, the increasing regulation of what we used to think of as private life, or personal relationships, not necessarily directly but indirectly by everything that the state and administrative organisation do. On the other hand, there is the intrusion into the public sphere of all those things that we used to think belonged to the private, including sexuality, personal relationships – the list is endless. The idea that you can neatly box this situation up in terms of public and private no longer seems to be true.

What are some of the implications of this arrival of difference? I agree very much with Anne Phillips point that this sometimes tempts people to say that, if one cannot assume homogeneity among British citizens any longer, one should begin to organise around differences. You could organise around differences if they were stable. The debate in political theory between individual and collective rights assumed that one could easily identify what the collective, or community, was. This suggests a notion of culture as rather fixed, rather stabilised.

This would be reasonable if we had a shift from homogeneity to difference. This has not occurred What we have is what is sometimes called in French 'différance'. 'Différance' is very different from difference, because it is that horrible mixture of some similarities and some differences, differences which refuse to remain the same. If you look inside the so-called ethnic communities you find incredible differentiation. The Asian population, for example, comes from such a variety of geographical, economic, religious, cultural and customary backgrounds as only to be recognisable as one group because *you* cannot tell the difference! Amongst themselves they know and recognise enormous differences. The differentiation within and between ethnic communities is running at an extremely rapid pace. For example, witness the fortunes and fates of those from the Indian community who are doing relatively well in education, who are beginning to hit the glass ceiling of promotion in professions in which they cannot advance and are beginning to migrate to their friends and relatives in Canada and the US. At the diametrically opposite end are the Bangladeshis in East London who are four times more disadvantaged on every measure you can think of than any other single population. So to speak of the ethnic minority, and to think of giving to ethnic communities plurally differentiated citizenship rights, is unthinkable. These are unstable changes. If you look across the generations, young people in each of these groups feel very differently from older people. They sometimes feel more at one with other young people in other ethnic groups, including the majority group, from which they are excluded than they do with some of their own parents. Yet sometimes they are drawn back into the parental relationship. What could a universal form of citizenship be, applied to a society which is pluralising in front of your eyes? What would it mean to say 'identical rights' or 'identical obligations', across this spectrum?

We all know this in our hearts, but whether we know it in political theory I doubt; whether we know it in educational theory I also doubt. My question is, what is it that we are not only going to do about this, but teach about it if we still want to hold the notion that equally just outcomes between citizens is one of the purposes of citizenship, and without that we should not talk about it? We have been involved in what I would call multicultural drift, sleepwalking into diversity. We do not actually know it is going on, we do not think it is the result of any planned process; it is a kind of unthinking sociological happening. We have just become multicultural, and we think, good liberal folk that we are, that because of this we have also become somehow quite tolerant about it. Multiculturalism thrives right alongside deep and fundamental forms of racism. One is not exclusive of the other. The celebration of the arrival of the Windrush, which told us how we have all over fifty years become a multicultural society, has to be put alongside the Macpherson Report on the Stephen Lawrence affair. This has shown that we have not become any different from how we were when the first battles arose in the streets between racists and the black community in 1958. I was present then, and I seem to have been present since then in informal enquiries, and the same perennial story has unrolled year after year after year.

These two things are happening together. We cannot delude ourselves that one is overcoming the other. Cultural differences do not open up. American feminist and political theorist Nancy Fraser makes a distinction between the politics of equality and the politics of recognition.[1] She establishes an unrealistic kind of absolute divide between the two. However, she is absolutely right to say that one of the changes that has been introduced in the political culture of advanced societies in the last 20 or 30 years is the increasing demand for recognition alongside, not replacing or displacing, the demand for equality. This of course leads to different kinds of demand, to different forms of politics, and to different kinds of education.

On the question of equality, the politics of recognition will not mean anything in the presence of yawning and growing gaps in equality between one group and another. The compounding of racial difference, ethnic difference and economic disadvantage, that triple disadvantage to which so many of the ethnic minority communities are subject, is a devastating one. To try to do something about it by saying you want to affirm, say, Bangladeshi identity without offering the opportunities of educational advantage, job opportunities, or retraining is a mirage in terms of citizenship.

I want to end by focusing on the second element in this, the recognition of difference. We pay too little attention to this in our discussions of citizenship, which are riveted by the ideas of universality and equality. One of the things the recognition of difference most profoundly requires is what I would call the skills of intercultural evaluation. If you live in a culturally plural society, in order not to be an administrator but to be an ordinary practising member of society at the lowest rank, you are going to have to constantly negotiate the inter-relationship between different cultural worlds which no longer exist in their primordial form, but which are already translated with one another. It is a very difficult situation to describe, but that is the situation we are in. People need the skills of intercultural evaluation, and if you want to know what might be a problem with intercultural evaluation I will give you one: would British society now, as it never has in the past, be willing to tolerate polygamy? If not, why not? Is serial monogamy quite so far away from organised polygamy as it used to be? It *is* different. I see men beginning to shudder, because serial monogamy means that you can transfer your responsibilities from one relationship to another. Whereas, unfortunately I have to tell you that organised polygamy requires you to look after all three wives at the same time, and you are legally, morally and religiously bound to do so! That explains one of the reasons why, just before they started burning Salman Rushdie's book, the *Mail* said we ought to look at the Muslim community because they are probably the only community that actually believes in family values.

Do not forget that, in an arena of life which is dominated by relative cultural values, it is no longer possible to say, once you go into the courts, exactly how to understand what is a common-sense interpretation of the events in front of you. The anthropologist Roger Ballard, is an expert on the Pakistani communities, and is able to give anthropological, legal advice to courts about how to understand the actions which are in front of them. This is happening now. What he says, in part, is that there is no systematic way in which the common law is taking up this question of cultural difference. However, it is no longer resting on the old assumption that it can simply apply the common-sense reasonableness of the man on the top of the Clapham omnibus in order to sort out the cultural relations between one set of people where the family is relatively attenuated, and another for instance, in the Asian communities, where the family is not only absolutely crucial but is a very different organisation, with a much wider kinship spread, probably integrated within the relationships of business. This is a different phenomenon altogether. The courts, very often asking about family crises that have developed around arranged marriages or around the position of women, need to sensitise themselves to the variety of cultural contexts that are in play.

That is at the everyday level. Clearly what it signals, at the national level, is some new way of beginning to negotiate what on earth it might mean to say all these different people are British, or feel they might be British – especially if they are British in a hyphenated rather than a singular way. What does it mean to say that, in the current crisis of British identity? British identity has been visibly in crisis for fifteen or twenty years. Euro-scepticism is a profound symptomatic indication of an uncertainty as to what it might mean to be British. This is occurring in an era when Britain is not the dominant power, is an offshore European island, no longer has an empire, and has suddenly discovered an ethnicity. It occurs in a world where its difference is already marked, where it is not the majority, not the norm against which difference is measured, but just another difference in the plurality of differences that make up an intricate globalised world.

Until we begin to accept the picture that I have been impressionistically trying to portray, we are not at the beginning of asking how our cultural institutions change in order to reflect this. Change is needed to avoid the dangers of formal pluralism while actually beginning to take on board, not in a drifting, unthinking way, but in a reflexive, serious and sustained way, how the institutions have to change as a consequence of cultural diversity. If we are not able to do that, what I want to know is, what the hell are you going to tell the kids about citizenship?

Endnote

1 Fraser, N (1997) *Justice Interruptus: Critical Reflections on the 'Post-Socialist' Condition* New York: Routledge

TOMORROW'S CITIZENS

Education and citizenship

Rabbi Jonathan Sacks
Nick Tate

5. The Judaic vision of citizenship education

Rabbi Jonathan Sacks

It is a great privilege to be able to contribute to this fascinating and crucially important debate. Let me begin by expressing my feelings in terms of that lovely story of the British philosophy professor who was invited to deliver a lecture on the metaphysics and epistemology of education in the University of Beijing. Not being entirely fluent in Mandarin, he was provided with a Chinese translator. He duly faced the large and impressive audience and began his lecture, and after the first sentence paused for the translator to render it into Chinese. But the translator shook his head and said, 'No, carry on – I'll tell you when I want you to stop.' This carried on for the second sentence and the third, in fact it carried on for 15 minutes. Finally the translator lifted up his hand and said four words in Chinese to the audience. The same happened for the next 15 minutes, and the next. Finally, at the end of the hour's lecture, the interpreter said three words to the audience and they all duly filed out. The English professor turned to the Chinese translator and said, 'I'm absolutely stunned that you were able to compress such a technical and elaborate lecture into so few words. Tell me, how did you do it?' And the interpreter said, 'It was very easy. After fifteen minutes I said, 'So far he hasn't said anything new.' After half an hour I said, 'He still hasn't said anything new.' After 45 minutes I said, 'I don't think he's going to say anything new', and after an hour I said, 'He didn't!''

On the issue of Education and Citizenship, I am not going to say anything new. On the contrary I am going to say something very old indeed, something that speaks to me from my tradition and that I hope will resonate with you.

I want to start with a moment that could not be more removed from current debates, but is not entirely irrelevant to them: one, which I consider a decisive moment, and a very often-overlooked one.

In the Biblical story of the Exodus, one aspect of it is almost invariably overlooked, as set out in the Hebrew Bible in chapters 12 and 13 of the Book of Exodus. Here is the scene: The Israelites are in exile in Egypt; they have been enslaved; they cry out for their freedom. Somehow, between them, God and Moses perform signs and wonders and eventually, after 210 years of suffering, they are about to go free. On the brink of their freedom Moses assembles the people and addresses them. The question is, what does he speak about? Let me ask you, what would *you* speak about? The perfect moment – here it is, one of the great moments of all time, here are the people about to leave captivity, and you are about to address them. What do you speak about? You could speak about many things. You could talk about freedom; about the destination, the land flowing with milk and honey; perhaps, if you were a realist, you could talk about the long journey that lies ahead across the wilderness – any one of those things would have been the great speech of a great leader.

What fascinates me is that Moses does none of those things. Instead, if you examine the biblical text, he does something very odd indeed, and something really quite visionary. He speaks three times about the distant future, and about children, and about handing the story on. 'It shall come to pass, when your children ask...so shall you say to them'. 'When your children say, in the future... This is how you shall answer'. 'You shall instruct your child on that day'. Three times, separately. There are the people thinking about freedom, and he is talking about education. They are thinking about tomorrow, he is thinking about the far distant future and generations to come. It is one of the strangest speeches in history, and surely one of the most profound. Because what Moses is saying is this: to defend the country you need an army, but to defend freedom you need education. You need families, and communities, and schools, in which the story is told and the values are transmitted across the generations, and it takes a long time. As one of our sages asserted, it took one day to get the Israelites out of Egypt and 40 years to get Egypt out of the Israelites.

Thereafter, education was set at the very heart of the Jewish vision of a free, inclusive and participative society. For more than three thousand years Jews became a people for whom their passion was study, their heroes were teachers, and the structure of Jewish communities in the Diaspora was of communities built around the schools.

Staying with this Book of Exodus, it contained an idea that I have not seen set forth very clearly in any work on political or educational theory, or indeed on Biblical interpretation. It constitutes the most radical insight I have come across on the relationship between education and citizenship. As far as the ancient people of Israel is concerned, the formative constitutional moment is in a sense one of the leading strands of western civilisation. It is set out in the Book of Exodus a little later on, in chapters 19 to 24, when the Israelites come to Mount Sinai; they see God revealed, they hear the Ten Commandments and they enact a covenant. At that moment Jews cease to become a people, linked only by an ancestry and shared suffering, and they become a body politic, under the sovereignty of God, whose written constitution is the Torah, the Book of the Covenant, the first constitution in history.

What is famous about that moment is what we call the Ten Commandments. However, the political structure is interesting and worth analysing. What happens is this: God tells Moses to go down to the people and make them an offer, tell them the political settlement he is about to propose, and only if they agree can he go ahead with the revelation. This is what Moses is to say – here are the words from Exodus, chapter 19: 'You have seen how I have brought you out of Egypt on eagles' wings and brought you to me. Now I wish to make you' and these words are crucial, '...a kingdom of priests in the holy nation'. The Bible emphasises that the Israelites agree, and it is only after their agreement that the revelation can proceed. The Bible actually says they agree 'with one voice', which is probably the first and last time that any Jews ever agreed about anything!

The first thing to notice about this moment, a moment which is no less important than Plato's *Republic* or Aristotle's *Ethics*, or his *Politics*, is its concept of citizenship. We know, through 20th century biblical scholarship, that the form of the covenant God makes with Israel is not unique. It is drawn from the language of diplomacy in the Near East, from the language of covenants between two political powers. What is unique are the parties to the covenant, which is worth reflecting on for a moment. The first and most interesting thing is that one of the parties is not a human ruler but God Himself. That is, God Himself is bound by a social covenant, a very revolutionary idea. The second, much more revolutionary, idea is that the other party to the covenant is not a ruler, as it is in every other ancient treaty we know. It is the people, the *demos*. The Bible persistently and repeatedly uses the phrase 'all the people'. The Bible is framing a radical political proposition, that there is no government without the consent of the governed, even if the governor happens to be the Creator of Heaven and Earth.

This is a very radical proposition. In the republic of faith everyone is a citizen on equal terms. It is open to debate whether or not the actual political structures that emerged in Israel ever lived up to this; the short answer is that they did not, and hence the existence of that famous personality type, the prophet, the divinely mandated critic of governments and the social status quo.

However, it is important to consider how such an idea is born. How is it possible that suddenly, somewhere in the world of ideas, is born as if out of nowhere the idea of a republic in which everyone is a citizen on equal terms? Here I want to focus attention on one phrase, the phrase from Exodus 19 that defines the Covenant: 'A kingdom of priests'. I want to suggest a radical reinterpretation, because I think those two words in Hebrew have been mistranslated for many centuries. We know that the most radical changes in the structures of society, changes indeed in the structure of consciousness itself, occur when there are changes in the way we record and transmit information. As a very simple example, without the technological breakthrough of printing, the Reformation would not have been possible.

It would be impossible to have a revolution that tells each individual to read his or her own Bible, and not rely on the authority of the Church, until you have a technology that allows private individuals, and not just churches, to have books. Without the invention of printing there could have been no Reformation, no redrafting of the political map of Europe, no birth of the modern. We are living through a second revolution probably greater than the invention of printing, namely the Internet, instantaneous global communication, which is certainly going to change our most basic human structures, our most basic definitions of what is a school, a university, a community, a nation.

However, of all these revolutions, the first and surely the greatest was the invention of writing. In Mesopotamia and Egypt some six thousand years ago it was that invention that made civilisation possible in the first place. The early forms of writing, cuneiform in Mesopotamia, hieroglyphics in Egypt, had one obvious problematic feature: each of the languages had too many symbols to be teachable or learnable by everyone. The result was that those societies, and every such society, had a cognitive élite, a small class who wrote. That meant by definition an extremely hierarchical society. Bacon was right to say 'Knowledge is power', for where knowledge is available only to the few, so too is power.

The crucial breakthrough came with the second invention, one that had profound political implications, the invention that happened approximately two thousand years later of the alphabet. For the first time a symbol set existed, reducible to something like 22 basic characters. The invention of the alphabet meant that for the first time one could record information in such a way that it was in principle readable by everyone. When that happens you can for the first time conceive of the possibility of a society without cognitive élites, where there is universal access to knowledge. If there is universal access to knowledge, there is equal access to power, to dignity, to citizenship. The first alphabets are what we know as the Semitic alphabets. They were found amongst that group of peoples – difficult to disentangle them at this distance – the Phoenicians, the Canaanites and the Hebrews, who lived in what was the land of Canaan between Mesopotamia and Egypt, and those alphabets appeared for the first time at around 2000 BC.

Prior to the invention of the alphabet, a very simple question remains; who was the knowledge class? Who could read and write? The priests. In ancient societies the priests were the guardians of knowledge. 'Hieroglyphic' means 'priestly script', much as the word 'clerical' in English means both a member of the clergy and somebody who can read and, much more importantly, write, because knowledge was associated with the priesthood. There is a revolutionary significance in the words 'A kingdom of priests'. I suggest that those words meant quite simply a society of universal literacy – the kind of society that is only conceivable after the technological breakthrough of the invention of an alphabet. A society in which, because everybody has access to knowledge, there is no knowledge class, no hierarchy. The word 'hierarchy' means 'an élite of priests'; there is no such élite because a kingdom of priests is one in which everyone is a priest, everyone can read and write. Because everyone can read and write, everyone has access to the laws, to the understanding of those laws, everyone is a citizen. And that is exactly what the prophet Isaiah means when he says: 'And all your children shall be students of God and great shall be the peace of your children', because they are participating members of a society. That is what Moses means when he says in what is for Jews the holiest of our prayers: 'And you shall teach these things diligently to your children, speaking of them when you sit at home, when you walk on the way, when you lie down, when you rise up.' Society is, for Judaism, a process of education.

This vision is an important and a distinctive one. It is in fact how Jewish societies tried to live, if not in early Biblical times at the very least in the days from the end of the Babylonian exile in the days of Ezra and Nehemiah two thousand years ago. According to this, education is not simply the transfer of information, it is not even the acquisition of skills; it is not even in the Aristotelian sense the harmonious or full development of the individual's personality. According to this, education is precisely the process of becoming a citizen. That is, becoming literate and articulate in the laws and narratives that constitute a society into which we are born and for which we carry collective responsibility.

And what is compelling about this vision is that it places education at the very heart of the society-building enterprise. What education is, in the Judaic vision, is a significant counter-force to the other two great and dominant factors in society: on the one hand, government, politics and the distribution of power; on the other hand, markets, economics and the distribution of wealth. There is one significant difference between those two and the realm of education, and the difference is simple: power on the one hand, wealth on the other, are at any given moment zero sum games. The more power I give away, the more money I give away, the less I have. The more I share it, the less I individually possess. Knowledge is precisely not a zero sum game. The best way to learn anything is to teach it. The more you give it away, the more you have; the more knowledge you share, the more you possess. That is why education allows us to resolve certain dilemmas that are never resolvable in politics and economics.

That is how Jewish communities lived for something like two and a half thousand years. Jews became a series of communities built around schools, academies and houses of study. You could see this instantly the moment you walked into a synagogue. Nowadays synagogues are not built this way, but if you walked into one in, say, Eastern Europe or Yemen a hundred years ago, you would instantly see the seats by the Eastern wall (the nearest thing we get to a House of Lords). And who sat in those seats? Not the people of wealth, nor of power, but the people of scholarship, informally recognised as such by the community. It was a community organised around education. That I find a genuinely compelling vision; education is the process by which each of us becomes an articulate member of a social order, which all of us own, which we inherit from the past, of which we are guardians for the future. Whose key values are subject to continuing debate, argument and reinterpretation. That is the Jewish vision.

Following, are some comments from that vantage point on where we stand today and where, hopefully, we will stand in the future. I just add these as little footnotes observations on how Britain today might fare on that kind of template.

First, we have not yet given education, or teachers, the dignity they deserve. They are the defenders of our civilisation more than any other class in society, and we deserve to honour our teachers.

The second point is that we haven't fully internalised the idea central to the Jewish vision that learning is an ongoing, life-long process. In Jewish law you have to start learning the moment you can speak, and you can stop learning the day you die. As an example, about fourteen years ago I was rushed to hospital for a big operation. I was just coming round from the anaesthetic when there was a knock on my door. It was a man in his late seventies, whom I vaguely recognised. He was holding a big volume of Talmud, and he said, 'I heard you were here. What a wonderful thing – now we can sit and learn together!'

Third, schools are not themselves independent variables. They cannot, in and of themselves, be agents of change. The Jewish community was always built around a tripartite structure: the home, the synagogue, the school – the reciprocal support of schools, families and communities. If that is missing, schools cannot do what we ask them to do, and if they fail to do it, that is not because they have failed us but because we have failed them.

Fourth, Jewish communities are set today, not in a traditional society but in a very untraditional society, surrounded by all sorts of cultural differences. These may be at odds with our values; the way of coping with this is to utilise the power of informal education. I remember sitting some years back with the entire staff of the Department of Education at the Hebrew University in Jerusalem. To get to know them I thought that, instead of asking them what they were researching on, I would give them an autobiographical question. I asked each of the members of staff what it was that led them to devote their life to Jewish education. They all gave the same answer – 'My youth group'. We had specialists in the room from every branch of education, pre-school, school, higher education, curriculum development, but none from youth groups – there was no specialist in informal education. We often find that those groups, run by the children themselves, are the best training we can give them in commitment, in leadership, in responsibility, in civic engagement. There is a downside to that – every Jew is a leader. The result is that we have some great leaders, but all too few followers!

Fifth, never underestimate the power of narrative in communicating citizenship. To give an obvious example, the most famous narrative that we have in Judaism is the Passover. We tell the story of the going out of Egypt, where we eat the bread of affliction, and taste the bitter herbs of slavery; that whole service was built around the questions of the youngest child at the table. That one phenomenon has meant that Jews can always be politically mobilised. Because, whether it is the story of the fight of blacks in South Africa, or the story today of Kosovan refugees, we instantly recognise that it is our story. We know it, we taste it, we feel it, we are one with it. Through that story, we can always mobilise our community for such things. Let me give you a non-Jewish example. We recently assembled an enormous gathering, some one and a half thousand people from around the world, for the 60th anniversary of the Kindertransport. In 1939, just before the outbreak of the Second World War, Britain allowed ten thousand Jewish children to come here from Germany and Austria. One of the non-Jewish families who brought two Jewish children into their home and adopted them were the parents of the film producer Richard Attenborough. At this gathering Lord Attenborough told the story of how his people adopted these two girls, whose own parents had been sent to the concentration camps, and how they became his sisters. It took five minutes, but I doubt if there was not any one of us in the room who was not weeping, or who did not leave the hall with their sense of moral possibilities enlarged, their moral ambitions uplifted. Stories change lives.

Sixth, when thinking about citizenship, never forget about the very close connection between giving and belonging. To take that example again of the Jews who came here in 1939 – what did they want? Obviously, when they first came they wanted just to live. But one thing they wanted above all, when they grew up, was to give back to society a little bit of what had been given to them. We explain that in language like 'reciprocity', or even more nobly in words like 'altruism'. But there is something deeper as well. A house in which I take refuge is one where I am a guest. A house that I help to build is one that I can call mine.

Social inclusion is a concept that cannot be fully translated into the language of rights. It is essentially related to the idea of participation. If I can say, 'I helped to make this,' then I can say, 'I belong', or as the Rabbis put it in a pun that really only works in Hebrew, 'Call them not 'your children' but 'your builders''. The best way of making children into citizens is to make them builders.

Lastly, of course, the single most important thing is for us, as parents and as citizens, is to give our children the space to grow. My three brothers and I all did fairly well academically. People used to ask my late father what he did to get four such clever sons, and he always used to say we took after our mother. My father came to this country at the age of five as a refugee from Poland. His family was very poor, and he had to leave school at the age of 14 to support the rest of the family. As a result he never had an education. And I will never forget what used to happen when I was four or five years old. I used to ask my father questions, and his reply was always the same: 'I never had an education, and so I can't answer your questions. But one day you will have the education that I never had, and one day you will teach me the answers to those questions.' Can you imagine the effect of that on a four year-old child? I was the size of a grasshopper, but I felt like a giant. Although I did become Chief Rabbi I will never become as good as my Dad was to me.

So that is my final proposition: children grow to be as big as the space we create for them, and that means believing in them, trusting in them, and above all taking pride in them, and if we do we too will achieve those lovely words of Wordsworth:

> What we love, others will love,
> And we will show them how.

6. Citizenship education in a liberal democracy

Nick Tate

It is a particular pleasure to be following the Chief Rabbi's contribution to this collection. One of the books on the relationship between the individual and the community that has impressed me most in recent years has been Dr Sacks's *The Politics of Hope*.[1] The thesis of his book is at the heart of the issues with which this volume is concerned.

The *Politics of Hope* distinguishes between liberal and libertarian views of a free society. Libertarian societies are ones where the state is morally neutral about the free choices which individuals make about their lives. Liberal societies are ones where the state is informed in its activities by a shared vision of the kind of civil society its citizens wish to promote, while respecting individual freedoms. Liberal societies attempt to preserve the gains of centuries of struggle to assert the rights of individuals, at the same time recognising that human beings are social animals who are only fully themselves through membership of a wider community.

The Chief Rabbi's thesis is that for much of the last fifty years, both here and in North America, we have inhabited a libertarian rather than a liberal culture. It is his hope that this is a trend that can be reversed. It is also his view that there are some areas where this may be already beginning to happen. In my view the proposals for citizenship education in schools form one of these areas.

On the assumption that the state is trying to promote the kind of liberal society I have just defined, three roles for the education system spring to mind.

First, it needs to help us find a way of combining our highly individualist culture, which emphasises autonomy and choice, with a reassertion of the place of community in our lives. As well as a vision of an educated person we also need a vision of a harmonious society – not a utopian one, but one in which there is a better balance between rights and responsibilities, between freedom and self-discipline, and in which there is a clearer sense of limits and of shared values. John Gray summed this up in his recent book *Endgames* as an 'individualism less possessive and more convivial' than we have at present, one that is balanced by 'the existence of a strong public culture, rich in options, and embodied in common institutions'.[2] The kind of school communities in which children are educated, and the ways they learn about their wider communities (including through citizenship education), can play a part in trying to shape such a society.

Second, we need to find ways of helping ourselves come to terms with a world in which identities are being recast under the impact of globalisation. 'Globalisation' of course is a contested concept and the extent to which we operate within a global economic (let alone cultural) system can be greatly exaggerated. Nevertheless, the current dominance of global market capitalism, alongside an unprecedented system of mass communication, places traditional civic and communal allegiances in a new light.

The third point is that one of the roles of the state in a liberal society is to support those institutions and ways of life – like the family – that promote these allegiances. Liberal states cannot be morally neutral about the culture of the societies they inhabit. Nor can schools.

This, however, gives us a problem in societies that have come to feel that values are personal, individual things, like tastes and preferences. Our values may appear to differ so fundamentally that there are few if any that we have in common any more. So the prime virtue – almost the only one we are all supposed to share – is to tolerate and respect other people's values whatever these might be. Such is the reaction against any kind of notion of moral authority that whenever one talks of education as the transmission of shared values someone invariably pops up in the audience to accuse one of indoctrination.

It was for this reason that the former School Curriculum and Assessment Authority set up its Values Forum and conducted its enquiry into the extent to which there were shared values within our society.[3] Its powerful, empirically based conclusion, was that indeed there were. We disagree about the source of our values and about their application to particular circumstances – moral rules frequently conflict – but there is a strong moral bedrock to our society which is shared by people of all faiths and none. It is these shared values that schools already aim to transmit. Schools are some of the most moral places in our society. They could not survive otherwise as communities. But what they need is greater support from the rest of society and the confidence that in transmitting, and in some cases strengthening, these values they are doing so on our behalf – in other words that *their* values are *our* values.

I am not advocating centrally imposed moral codes, but I do support an explicit recognition that education has a moral purpose; that there are such things as shared values (and indeed 'virtues') which help to define our society; and that some values are non-negotiable.

In the same way that the state should not be morally neutral about the culture of the wider society so it should not be morally neutral about the need to support minority cultural and religious communities within its midst. The sign of a civilised state is that it respects the allegiances that individuals have to communities other than the overall community of the nation-state, except where these conflict. This is something to which the whole curriculum needs to be sensitive. It is also at the heart of what we are trying to do in citizenship education.

But what are we trying to do in citizenship education? My organisation, the Qualifications and Curriculum Authority (QCA), was charged, statutorily, with consulting on the Secretary of State's proposals for a new subject called 'Citizenship'. We also consulted on his proposals for a linked framework for personal, social and health education. During consultations of this kind we were required to be dispassionate and simply listen. We have presented our advice to the Secretary of State, suggesting whatever changes to the proposals we felt were warranted in the light of consultation, and publishing our recommendations and consultation report.

Our current citizenship initiatives need to be placed in an international perspective, drawing on one of QCA's most interesting current research projects – the International Review of Curriculum and Assessment Frameworks Project carried out on our behalf by the National Foundation for Educational Research.[4] This has been looking at curriculum and assessment frameworks in 16 countries. In addition to England these include the US, Commonwealth countries (Australia, Canada and New Zealand), our main partners within the European Union, a country emerging from communism (Hungary), and three countries from South-East Asia and the Pacific Rim. Values, aims and the place of citizenship education within the curriculum have been a major focus of study.

The project has highlighted the close links between citizenship education, the social, cultural, economic and political structures of the countries in question, and the changes taking place within these structures. Whether implicitly or explicitly, consciously or unconsciously, the different aims and provision of citizenship education reflect the values, priorities and concerns of the education systems of which they are a part. Crucially, citizenship education tells one something about what a society feels it stands for and what it wants as a result to transmit through its education system. It is partly because so many societies are asking themselves these questions with such urgency at the present time that citizenship education is of interest worldwide. Some of the pressures encouraging them to do so are common to many of the countries in our sample: the impact of economic globalisation (I use this term with the caveats mentioned earlier); the worldwide impact, linked to economic globalisation, of a largely US-based mass culture; the development of regional structures such as the European Union; internal pressures for devolution and autonomy; concerns within democracies about growing civic disengagement. Other pressures, however, are highly distinctive of particular societies.

I recently visited one of the countries in our sample – France – to find out about their education minister's reform programme for the lycées. This involves the introduction for the first time of a compulsory programme of *éducation civique, juridique et sociale*. Intended to extend across all three years of the lycée, for all 15-18 year olds, this has been introduced in the first of these years from September 1999. It will build on the *éducation civique* which already exists for younger children. Talking to people involved in the introduction of this programme – and in particular to Bernard Crick's equivalent, Jacques Guin – it became clear that the pressures for such a move come from a variety of directions: the need to clarify identities at a time when France's relationships with Europe, with the francophone world and with a US and English language-dominated global culture and economy are developing rapidly; the need to redefine and re-transmit a republican citizenship which incorporates the cultural diversity of modern France; the need to tackle the violence and incivility affecting many communities, especially in the poorer suburbs of large cities; the need, for all young people, in an increasingly complex and fluid society, to develop values, attitudes and skills essential for their future effectiveness as workers, citizens and human beings; and, last but not least, the political commitment of the responsible minister to do something urgently, through citizenship education, to try and meet these needs. Some of these pressures are similar to ones we experience here. Others are distinctively French.

Citizenship education moulds itself to the contours of the society within which it is taking place. This is especially so when aims that on paper look alike are translated into provision within a particular education system. I was struck, looking at existing programmes for 11-13 year olds in French schools, at the particular emphasis on liberty, equality and fraternity, on the laicity of the state, and on European citizenship. Key documents highlighted for reference include ones of iconic significance in the formation of a French civic identity: the 1789 Declaration of the Rights of Man, the constitution of the Fifth Republic and, as a classic text on equality, Victor Hugo's *Les Misérables*. It came as no surprise that responsibility for civic education rests largely with teachers of history, and to some extent geography, and that this is the pattern that will be replicated in the lycées.

Our international survey quoted an earlier classification of approaches to citizenship education as points on a 'minimal-maximal' continuum. 'Minimal' interpretations of citizenship education were described as exclusive, formal, content led, didactic and with outcomes that were easier to measure. 'Maximal' interpretations, by contrast, were inclusive, process led, values based, interactive and with outcomes that were more difficult to measure. On this classification France appears to find its place towards the 'minimal' end of the continuum while our current proposals in England might be described as at the 'maximal' end. I am dubious, however, about reifications of this kind. Not just are the terms 'minimal' and 'maximal' used in a way which, unhelpfully, mixes description and value judgement, but differences in relation to such varied areas as aims, content and assessment are impossible to place on any kind of overarching continuum. Both English and French proposals, for example, are concerned with content and process, but in ways that reflect their different societies. It is quite compatible to want children to learn about the constitution of the Fifth Republic and the Declaration of the Rights of Man (or, in this country, about universal suffrage and the role of parliament), and to see the development of a particular civic society as a story that needs to be told, while at the same time promoting values and attitudes and direct civic involvement at a local level. David Blunkett's proposals, like those of Claude Allègre in France, are intended to achieve both.

One of the advantages of international comparisons is that it makes you look at your own country's arrangements in a new light. It also encourages a more global view. The results of QCA's curriculum and assessment frameworks project lead me to try and identify the 'big ideas' behind our own citizenship education initiative, to clarify these and to consider the best ways of getting them across. The rest of this chapter will suggest what some of these 'big ideas' might be.

One weakness of the present version of the national curriculum is that it tells teachers what they have to teach but fails to tell them why. We have been addressing this deficiency as part of our current revisions, through an introductory statement of values and aims, and through attempts to define the contribution of each subject to the overall education of the child and how this develops across the different phases of schooling. If teachers are able to develop a shared sense of what a particular subject is for they are more likely to teach it well than if they are simply following a prescribed set of procedures. Where they have been captured by a 'big idea' – such as the big ideas behind the national literacy and numeracy strategies and the national targets, or the simple but powerful and novel idea that schools should be striving each year to do better than their previous corporate best – great things are possible, as we are beginning to see in schools at the present time.

What, then, are these 'big ideas' in citizenship education? I will suggest seven of them. First, citizenship is about values. The rationale for citizenship education asserts the following values: that it is a good thing to be active citizens; that it is important to be informed, critical and responsible; that we have duties; that we should respect other people's identities, and that it is a good thing to be reflective. Citizenship education is about promoting and transmitting these values, which are the shared values of our society. It is not morally neutral about the kind of society we want to establish in this country, or about the kind of government – a participative democracy – that we want to encourage, or about what it is to be a fully developed and good human being. We have always striven in education to promote these things, but there has been a curious reluctance in recent years – arising from the currents of moral relativism I mentioned earlier – to state unequivocally that this is what we are trying to do. The time has come to put all that behind us. In doing so, we need to be clear that promoting certain fundamental values does not involve promoting applications of those values that are widely contested within our society. We want people to be critical and reflective, but we are morally neutral as educators, at least in non-denominational schools, about the conclusions they may reach on contested issues such as abortion, euthanasia, genetically modified food, the reform of the House of Lords or the pros and cons of political conservatism, Marxism or European federalism. In all these areas citizenship education is about facilitating choices – and in many cases choices that will be made later in life – not about prescribing them. Citizenship education, like all good education, is the opposite of indoctrination.

Second, citizenship education is about helping young people, both now and later in life, to make sense of and to begin to shape their own identities. We hear a great deal about identity these days. I myself have talked quite a bit over the years about its role in education. This has always been important. It is even more so now given the fluidity of the world under the impact of rapid economic and cultural change. In this country we are facing issues about the changing relationship between our identities as inhabitants of England, Britain, Europe and the world. Devolution within the United Kingdom, the increasingly diverse (but also at the same time, in other ways, increasingly homogeneous) nature of English society, changing relationships between Northern Ireland and the Irish Republic, our evolving membership of the European Union and of the Commonwealth, our close cultural ties with a very powerful and all pervasive US-based global mass culture, the impact of economic globalisation – all these are compelling us to feel and think again about own identities. To find our way through this moral and cultural maze young people need a range of knowledge, skills, values and attitudes that schools, parents and the wider community all have a crucial role in providing. Citizenship education is not the only part of the school curriculum to contribute to this task. It has a particularly important responsibility, however, in enabling young people to understand their identities as members of the civic communities – local, national and European – in which they have duties and rights. One of its key themes must be the inclusiveness of civic, as distinct from cultural, religious or ethnic, identity, and the idea that it is perfectly acceptable, indeed normal and in many cases essential, to have multiple identities: to be English and British, to be British and Jamaican, to be Muslim and European. The Secretary of State's proposals are quite explicit that understanding about these multiple identities is an important part of citizenship education.

Third, citizenship education is about participation. One of its main aims is that people, as a result, should be active and become involved. It is Aristotelian in that it takes for granted that people are more likely to achieve their potential as human beings if they play an active part in the communities to which they belong. This does not mean that everyone is being encouraged to join political parties, lobby for local causes and run the neighbourhood watch. But it does involve an assumption that a wholly individualistic, hedonistic and inward looking life is less than complete. This assumption is taken for granted as one of our shared values.

A particular role for citizenship education, as the proposals state, will be for pupils to 'be taught about the importance of voting'. Given the low figures for young people's participation in the 1997 general election, and the recent dismal turnout at local and European elections, this must be a central task for citizenship education in the coming years. But I am well aware that the solutions do not lie solely, or indeed mainly, with schools.

Fourth, citizenship education is not just about rights. It is also, and principally, about duties. Human rights are important; people need to learn about them; rights need to be defended; rights often need to be strengthened; but we have heard so much about them in recent years that we have sometimes come to forget that at the other side of the coin are duties. We have somehow developed a public image of human life which is all about self-creation, self-satisfaction, the pursuit of pleasure, doing one's own thing – the 'me-society' – which is very different both from the reality of people's everyday lives and what we instinctively feel life, properly lived, ought to be like. We need to redress the balance. Quite how we do this in education, in ways that are not didactic or hypocritical, is a considerable challenge and one that requires great subtlety of approach, particularly with adolescents.

Fifth, citizenship education is the responsibility of the whole school community, including parents, not just of those teachers particularly charged with its implementation. Although defined in our proposed new national curriculum as a subject, it is a very distinctive subject whose provisions have implications for every teacher in a school. Unlike France, which prescribes how much time should be spent on civic education and which teachers (history and geography teachers) should teach it, we will not be statutorily requiring schools to spend a particular amount of time on citizenship education. Indeed the Secretary of State is proscribed by legislation from doing so in the case of national curriculum subjects. Nor will we be requiring it to be taught in a particular way. There are, and will be, many ways of meeting the proposed requirements. They will all, however, involve a level of commitment across the whole school community. They will also all involve, in my view, some separately allocated provision, whether or not attached to other subjects. The track record of teaching subjects in a wholly cross-curricular way does not encourage me to feel that we will meet our objectives if this is the only way in which we try and teach citizenship. It will also be essential to ensure the closest links with history and geography, especially up to the age of 14 when these subjects cease to be compulsory, and with personal, social and health education. History teaching in the past has sometimes been too detached from its role in preparing young people for citizenship. We need history to help young people understand how the world we live in today is a continuing part both of 'our island's story' (and indeed of our islands' stories) – stories full of diversity and complexity – and of a European and a world story as well. I hope that revisions to the national curriculum will help to strengthen history teachers' conception of this role.

Sixth, we need to get across the message that citizenship education is about an appropriate balance between knowledge, understanding, skills, values and attitudes and that its success will depend on the interaction of all of these elements. This is where the 'minimal – maximal' continuum I referred to earlier is quite helpful. We do not want citizenship education that is mostly or largely a matter of learning content. On the other hand we also do not want citizenship education that is simply about developing skills and attitudes in some kind of cultural and political vacuum. There is a continuing debate about the balance between these various elements right across our education system. The greatest danger at the moment, in my view, comes from those who have got into the habit of feeling that knowledge somehow does not really matter. It does and, as my colleague Ted Wragg says, the more knowledge there is the more of it we need to know.

Seventh, we need to get across that we are serious about citizenship education. This government has succeeded in getting across the message that it is serious about education. It has also, through co-ordinated strategies, got across key specific messages about literacy and numeracy in primary schools, and about continuous corporate self-improvement for all educational institutions. A co-ordinated effort will also be needed for citizenship education when it becomes statutory from September 2002. Bernard Crick's report contained the following sentence: 'we aim at no less than a change in the political culture of this country both nationally and locally.'[5] That is an ambitious aim and to get anywhere near to achieving it will require a co-ordinated campaign extending far beyond education. We will need guidance. We will need case studies. We will need the support of business and voluntary bodies. We will need public figures to be associated with the initiative. We will need to give thought to ways of accrediting and rewarding those aspects of citizenship capable of assessment. We will need professional development. QCA very much looks forward to working with the government in helping to make this a reality.

Endnotes

1 Sacks, J (1997) *The Politics of Hope* London: Jonathan Cape

2 Gray, J (1997) *Endgames: Questions in Late Modern Political Thought* Cambridge: Polity Press

3 SCAA (1996) *National Forum for Values in Education and the Community: Consultation on Values in Education and the Community* London: Schools Curriculum and Assessment Authority

4 O'Donnell, S, Le Métais, J, Boyd, S and Tabberer, R (1998) *INCA: the International Review of Curriculum and Assessment Frameworks Archive* (CD-Rom) Second edition London: Qualifications and Curriculum Authority Values Forum of School Curriculum and Assessment Authority

5 Advisory Group on Citizenship (1998) *Education for Citizenship and the Teaching of Democracy in Schools* London: Qualifications and Curriculum Authority

TOMORROW'S PRACTICE

Teachers, schools and civic learning

Bernard Crick
Charles Clarke MP
Jenny Talbot
William Atkinson
Martin Cross

7. The Citizenship Order for schools

Bernard Crick

> We aim at no less than a change in the political culture of this country both nationally and locally: for people to think of themselves as active citizens, willing, able and equipped to have an influence in public life and with the critical capacities to weigh evidence before speaking and acting; to build on and to extend radically to young people the best in existing traditions of community involvement and public service, and to make them individually confident in finding new forms of involvement and action among themselves.[1]

The concept of citizenship and its history has, in the last decade, attracted much academic debate – as other contributions to this book have shown. The debate has often been of a very high standard. Political thinking is not dead, as one might sometimes think when one reads even the quality press or considers the terms in which most political debate is conducted; but it has locked itself up, or been locked up where it can do no harm, in the ivory tower. Moreover, despite the focus of academic debate on democratic principles, institutions and the practices of a free citizenry, there has been an astonishing lack of academic interest in this country in what must be one of the essential conditions for the universal practices of free citizenship: education, specifically the period of compulsory school education of all our nation's children.[2]

Since 1989 we have had a compulsory national curriculum for all local authority schools, but Citizenship was not a required subject. There was an excellent advisory paper on Citizenship as a cross-curricular theme, if any school cared to take it on; but few did so in any systematic or intellectually coherent manner. What is surprising about the Secretary of State's Citizenship Order of 1999 is not its existence, but that it came so late on the educational scene:[3] that it was not required in the 1988 legislation. The then Secretary of State for Education, Kenneth Baker, was known to favour it.[4] Perhaps he judged that it would have meant too much innovation and prescription all at once, or perhaps he was overruled by his Prime Minister. But more fundamentally many leading politicians and headteachers felt that there was no need for citizenship to be taught as a subject; all that was needed resided in the *ethos* of a good English school. The traditionalist version of this ethos was, of course, an idealised picture of independent schools, and an outdated one at that: an ethos that had produced *good leaders* – officers in the Empire and the two world wars, colonial administrators, public servants, clergy and responsible landowners – whereas, in fact, most of their products were now heading for the city of London, not even for industry. The progressive version of this (happily more prevalent in print than in sobering practice) was the democratic school, an ethos of experience and example that rendered both the formal teaching of Citizenship redundant and, in extreme cases of self-delusion, formal teaching of any kind. As so often, extremes live off each other and distort public perceptions of normal, mundane, moderate professional practice. As Orwell once said, the Peace Pledge Union was a product of the Navy League.

Traditionalism stressed an ideal of *good citizenship* (obeying the law without question and giving up one's seat to elders on the underground); and progressivism stressed an ideal of *active citizenship* (trying to change unjust laws, trying to democratise voluntary bodies, even the occasional demo and aggressive non-violent protest). Obviously I parody some well-known good intentions to argue that neither will do by itself, that both are needed in sensible combination.

A new consensus that Citizenship should be taught and learnt has come about as part of a general questioning of whether our old institutions serve the purposes of society and worries about the alienation of young people from public values. Low voting turnout among the young is only one measure of this. To my mind, even more significant, is the low level of participation of young people in voluntary bodies. Yes, splendid examples to the contrary can be found, and they are heartening reminders of what is possible. But in number they disappoint grievously. Change will not come of itself.

In the 1970s some of us were trying to promote programmes in schools with the object of enhancing what was cleverly called 'political literacy' – the knowledge, skills and values needed to be an informed, active and responsible citizen.[5] But, in hindsight, that was too narrowly political – or could encourage a narrowing sense of what counted as political. 'Political literacy' can be needed in almost any form of group activity, and even the skills needed for party activity or pressure group activity may best be learned in local voluntary groups and, indeed, in discussions of real issues and the exercise of real responsibilities in school.

The terms of reference for the advisory group on 'Education For Citizenship and the Teaching of Democracy in Schools' asked us 'To provide advice on effective education for citizenship in schools — to include the nature and practices of participation in democracy; the duties, responsibilities and rights of individuals as citizens; and the values to individuals and society of community activity'. It is the implications of that last phrase that broadens the concept from political education into citizenship education. Some may suspect a mere politic play with words in this: parents favour the idea of citizenship education but not political education.[6] But there is classic political philosophy behind this shift. Did not De Tocqueville famously argue that the very foundations of liberty depend on 'corporations' or self-governing groups of any kind as intermediary between the state and the individual? Edmund Burke extolled 'the small platoon' as pillar of the state. And Aristotle had argued that, if a tyrant was to be secure, he must destroy all such groups, however unpolitical they are, because it is participation in small social groups that creates mutual trust between individuals, without which any opposition to tyranny (or may one say to misgovernment in general?) is futile.

To come down to earth. There is now to be a new subject called Citizenship in secondary schools – statutory, therefore required and prescribed in an order. It rests on three operative ideals:

> Firstly, children learning from the very beginning self-confidence and social and moral responsible behavior, both in and beyond the classroom, both towards those in authority and towards each other... Secondly, learning about and becoming helpfully involved in the life and concerns of their communities, including learning through community involvement and service to the community... Thirdly, pupils learning about and how to make themselves effective in public life through knowledge, skills and values – what can be called 'political literacy', seeking for a term that is wider than political knowledge alone.[7]

There is also to be a new non-statutory subject in primary schools, PSHE and Citizenship (personal, social and health education) for which guidance is being drawn up, not compulsory but likely to be taken seriously by the inspectorate, even when some schools are not enthused.

My advisory group was unanimous in recommending that Citizenship become statutory in secondary schools. The history of take-up for voluntary cross-curricular guidance papers was not a happy one. Also the very idea of democratic citizenship is a universal one. It must be a universal entitlement. Admittedly one can take a horse to water but it may not drink. But the civic drink must be a universal entitlement, clearly there for all. The Government has accepted that. If any Ministers had doubts and might have thought that the Report's recommendations should be on offer to schools but not compulsory, three considerations prevailed. One, education for citizenship in schools and FE colleges is a necessary condition for the success of constitutional reform, if part of its object is gradually to create a more participative, self-sustaining and genuinely democratic society. Two, education for citizenship in schools and FE colleges is a necessary condition for a more inclusive society, or for helping to diminish exclusion from schools, cynicism, apathy, petty criminality and vandalism, and a kind of could-not-care-lessitude towards voting and public issues among young people. Three, we are a democracy, however imperfect, and its legal citizens should know how it works and how it could be improved if we could change our collective mentality from being subjects of the Crown to being both good and active citizens.

You will find that the strong, bare bones of the new Citizenship Order either directly follow from, or are consistent with, the main thrusts of the Report of the advisory group. Being a statutory order, that is to say a legally enforceable document, it contains only a formal statement of aims and only an implied justification; it carries no advice about methods of delivery, learning techniques nor teaching methods appropriate to Citizenship. Such advice will follow, as is customary, from the QCA. But it will only be advice and, like the Order itself, will not specify details of what is to be taught, and how. The virtue of the Order is that the generality of its prescriptions will leave the school and the teacher with a good deal of freedom and discretion, possibly more than in the other statutory subjects.

This has occurred, I think, for two reasons: firstly, it would not be appropriate for either the government (through the DfEE) or a central quango (the QCA) to give precise prescriptions on some politically sensitive matters. The detail should be at arms' length from the state: it will be for Ofsted, LEA advisers and governors to watch for bias or bad teaching. Secondly, in the very nature of citizenship there must be local discretion. Hence the order is what David Blunkett has called 'a light touch order', or what I have just called 'strong, bare bones'. The schools will not be given ready-made lessons by either DfEE or QCA, nor told which 'events, issues and problems' should be discussed. If some teachers look for lessons off the peg, they will find a variety on offer from various independent bodies from which to pick and mix – notably the Citizenship Foundation, Community Service Volunteers (CSV) Council for Education in World Citizenship (CEWC) and the Institute for Citizenship. These are likely to be the principle providers of flesh on the bones, either in print or on the National Grid for Learning. Other bodies too will feed in on the parts of the order that touch on human rights, race relations, consumer rights, financial literacy and global concern. The Order allows for considerable flexibility. What is not ruled in is not ruled out. So long as everything in the Order is covered to achieve a basic understanding, some topics, such as global citizenship, human rights or ethnic understanding, can be stressed more than others.

I have said that, in the main, the Order follows the Report. The two must be read together, especially in relation to the teaching and discussion of 'events, issues and problems' – even if the Report says 'controversial' and the Order more quietly says 'contemporary events, issues and problems'. But in two respects the Order goes radically further than the Report. The Report strongly recommended, as good practice but not as part of a statutory order, pupil participation both in school and in the local community. In relying on good practice rather than compulsion we thought we were being politically prudent (always a virtue in my opinion).[9] And enough was enough for the time-being. We were acutely aware of the dangers of appearing to overload the bending backs of so many teachers. But the Secretary of State sent word to the working party who were drafting the consultative order (civil servants, QCA, teachers, advisers) that actual participation could be mandatory. We did not demure. Colleagues were amused that for once I had underplayed a strong hand. Half a cake would not have been better than none. Without the experiential, participative side of Citizenship learning, some schools could turn the brave new subject into safe and dead, dead safe, old rote-learning Civics. There is an awful lot that could be learnt and assessed about, say, local government law.

The aim of the new subject is to create active and responsible citizens. There was a philosophy behind the Report, of course: what scholars call civic republicanism – a term not yet current in political discourse; but also a kind of pluralism. Pupils (indeed each one of us – never too late to learn) must be encouraged to find and formulate their own values, but to recognise that in the United Kingdom (let alone Europe and the outside world beyond) there is a diversity of values, national, religious, regional and ethnic. Some of these we have in common, some not. We must learn to respect the values of all others equally; but respect (as John Rawls has maintained) neither implies agreement nor equality of praise. Put in another way, my late friend Ernest Gellner was fond of saying 'social tolerance always, intellectual tolerance never.' A bit harsh? In dealing with the young (even with students) we learn to correct error and work against prejudice gently – firmly, but gently.

The Order, of course, applies only to England. But the curriculum it enjoins covers knowledge of the diversity of the four nations, the United Kingdom as a whole. If our children had some recognition from an early age that their England is part of a multi-national United Kingdom, respect for other forms of diversity, religious and ethnic – so commonly misnamed racial – would be easier. What we have in common, what holds this diversity together, are the values and practices of a common citizenship. Yes, Citizenship in schools has a wide agenda and needs to have. Its success will be difficult to measure for many years, for the real measures will not be assessments of performance in a subject matter, whether written or oral, but will be the consequences for social behaviour. This is neither easily measureable nor predictable in the short term. But it is common sense to make the big effort, at long last. We can no longer afford not to try.

Endnotes

1 Advisory Group on Citizenship (1998) *Education for Citizenship and the Teaching of Democracy in Schools* London: Qualifications and Curriculum Authority

2 An exception is Derek Heater who knows schools as well as the academy and has mastered the literature of the former to the

advantage of latter. See his most recent book Heater (1999) *What is Citizenship*? London: Polity

3 A good summary of the past is in Kerr, D (1999) *Re-Examining Citizenship Education* Slough: National Foundation for Educational Research, with a comprehensive bibliography

4 When Kenneth Baker was chairman of the Hansard Society the report of a working party was published as, Crick, B and Porter, A (1978) *Political Education and Political Literacy* London: Longman. He argued strongly in an interview with the then Secretary of State, Shirley Williams, for government money for in-service training – the working party's priority. But being close to a general election, she sent us away with funding for something less contentious that we had not asked for, research into assessment. It would not be proper for me to relate what he said as we left together

5 The Hansard programme (*ibid*) began to have widespread take-up in schools just before the change of government; then followed its slow decline, often demise; but many of its principles and suggested methods are still relevant

6 A Mori poll commisioned and published by the Institute for Citizenship (1998) *Public Attitudes Towards Citizenship* London: Institute for Citizenship, showed 90 per cent support for Citizenship to be taught, albeit – I suspect – most members of the public perceive the term primarily in the 'good citizenship' sense rather than the 'active citizenship' and political literacy sense. But there was over eighty per cent support from parents and governors in Mori's evaluatiion for QCA of the widespread consultation on *The Secretary of State's Proposals*, which the sample and the respondents would have received and presumably read and understood its full width and import

7 Advisory Group on Citizenship *op cit*

8 Literally in my book (1962) *In Defence of Politics* London: Penguin/Weidenfield, now put out of print (except in the US) just when teachers might find it of interest

8. Creating listening schools

Charles Clarke MP

Why do we need education for citizenship? The starting point for any discussion has to be the fact that modern society is very complex and changing fantastically rapidly, much more rapidly than it changed during the childhood of my generation. The changes are obviously economic (we live in a global economy), technological, social, and environmental; a range of processes of massive change. The increasing rapidity of change creates difficulties not only for our generation but also in particular for our children. Our parents had different, vital challenges, but this issue of change is on our agenda and our children's in a way that it never has been before.

Individuals in such circumstances have to be able to adapt to survive economically and socially. They have to be able to master that process of change rather than be its victims. That is the central challenge which the whole of our education system faces at the moment. It is obvious that those who are poorly educated lack the confidence and skills to take advantage of the new opportunities, and will find life increasingly difficult. They in particular will be at the whim of this massive process of change. They will have difficulty even in finding employment and sustaining an income, let alone being able to play a wider role in understanding and controlling the world in which they live.

The Government is working hard to help schools improve standards right across the board. It is important to emphasise that basics like literacy and numeracy are a precondition for effective participation in this new world. At the same time it is crucial to acknowledge that education for life is far broader than those particular skills, vital though they are. The fact is that, in this process of change, children are exposed to a very wide range of complex personal, social and moral issues as they grow up; from basics like managing personal money, personal relationships, and keeping safe, to dealing with current local, national and international developments. On television screens every night, children are blasted with a range of subjects which pose difficult and complicated issues for them to address, and it is important for them to feel equipped to handle them.

The range of these issues was reflected in a recent MORI poll, commissioned by the Qualifications and Curriculum Authority, of secondary school pupils.[1] It showed that they did want better teaching about relationships, preparing for parenthood, and managing money. They also prioritised a range of issues about the political process, the decision-making system in which they worked, and their ability to participate in democracy. This government believes that education for citizenship, alongside personal, social and health education, should help pupils to think for themselves and make sense of their own lives as they prepare for adulthood. Such education should facilitate their understanding of how they as individuals relate to the community of which they are a part. I would define 'community' broadly. It includes the environment, the political process, the decision-making structure of which they are a part, in a society that is more diverse and culturally rich than ever before.

Part of the process of education for citizenship is the need to develop in all young people a sense of belonging, and the skills and motivation to want and be able to make a difference to their own lives and the lives of their communities. That is the only way in which we can build an inclusive society. It is the only way in which we can avoid the types of alienation that have disfigured parts of our society over recent decades. People are increasingly feeling that they have no stake in the future and no ability to control it. For all those reasons we need education for a new citizenship. The case to develop citizenship as part of our National Curriculum needs to be understood in that context, as a critical part of equipping our children to deal with the process of change that is taking place.

A central element of this requirement is the need to develop civic values: rights and responsibilities, diversity and social justice. Human and legal rights are the very basis of a civilised society. Children and young people need to know about the concept of human rights and responsibilities first and foremost. They have to understand where it is possible and appropriate for them to intervene in society, what their responsibilities are to society, how those issues relate in often complex circumstances. So citizenship is about moral and social responsibility; it is about making difficult moral choices, and it is about asserting the will of everybody, whatever our different circumstances, to live together and resolve differences constructively. It involves creating an anti-bullying culture in school; addressing harassment; and stopping a culture that encourages drug taking in schools, or creates a climate where teenage pregnancies can develop. It means improving school attendance and reducing exclusions. It needs to address the whole climate of a school, to ensure that its culture is a listening one; one that asserts and respects the rights and responsibilities of everybody, and is rigorous in opposing bullying and harassment that exclude certain people from full participation in the school.

A society such as ours, multi-cultural, multi-faith, multi-lingual and multi-ethnic, needs to have forms of citizenship which respect and value this diversity. This was clearly highlighted by the Macpherson enquiry into the tragic death of Stephen Lawrence, which rightly gave a prominent role to education and the importance of addressing that through the National Curriculum.[2] As an individual who has recently moved from inner city London to Norwich, I feel it is crucial to refute the idea that these problems do not exist in rural communities such as Norfolk. In many inner cities these problems are being addressed, whereas in other parts of the country they are not prioritised in the way they need to be.

Education can and should do more to promote social justice in our communities. Citizenship, alongside PSHE and other aspects of school life, plays a major part in helping to create a culture of tolerance, understanding and respect for all, irrespective of their gender, race, culture, colour or religion. Such a culture is a precondition to building and sustaining an environment in which learning can flourish for all pupils; an environment where the self-confidence and self-esteem of every pupil can be built up and strengthened.

Education for the new citizenship, aimed at developing citizenship skills, is at the core of the government's approach to these matters. The word I use, which may not exist in the dictionary, is 'articulacy'. It is particularly important for young people, as they grow up, to be able to articulate their views in a number of different ways: on paper, orally, in a variety of different types of environment which involve respecting what others are saying as well as self-expression. In that context I welcome some of the initiatives that have been taking place, for example the 'Listening to Children' initiative organised by some of the major charities.

Education for citizenship will encompass knowledge about political and social institutions, and parliamentary government, which is absolutely essential. It is important that people understand how decisions are taken, what the nature of those decisions is, the constraints on them, the way they operate, and most importantly the way people can play a part in them.

However, I do believe that the agenda has to be broader than that. It must help pupils to develop the capacity to manage their own lives, and take an active part in their communities. It must provide opportunities for children and young people to develop the confidence, personal and social skills to express themselves well, so that they are able to take greater control of their own lives. It is about encouraging responsibility and respect for rules and laws, whilst developing the knowledge and skills to change laws in a peaceful and responsible way. It is about giving practical experience of exercising responsibility. Schools should be encouraged to give their pupils a say in real responsibility, through effective school councils, involvement in drawing up and managing schools' anti-bullying policies, peer support schemes, and self-managed projects which make a real difference to their lives and those of their communities.

Many schools are already doing these things and more, very successfully and very creatively. In a First School about a hundred metres from where I live, philosophy classes are being organised for four to eight year-olds. These lessons aim to encourage them to think critically, to ask questions, to listen actively to others, to analyse and discuss real issues across the curriculum, to offer deeper understanding which leads to better academic performance and better co-operation between pupils, all of which are good citizenship skills. I visited this school to listen to a class of five year-olds, and saw how a simple conversation on personal likes and dislikes can easily lead to a powerful discussion, with the idea that children have the right to say what they think and respect others in that process.

South Camden Community School is running a peer education project involving Bengalis, Somalis, Nigerians and Eritreans in tackling problems of violence in school, and taking their message into the community. Fairoaks School in Hampshire has a very lively school council, tackling real and practical matters. Pupils hold regular surgeries, undertake research, and write and distribute 6,000 copies of their newspaper to the school and its local community. Mill Chase Community School, also in Hampshire, uses different areas of the curriculum, Art, History and Languages, to enhance citizenship. The pupils themselves have created an interactive website to explore racism and other issues with pupils in European schools. (This is an example of the real power of ICT and websites in developing many of these points in schools, and it is growing fast.)

Pupils across the country are working out safe routes to school, which cut down car use and pollution, and comparing them with other schools through the Young Transmit website run by the National Children's Bureau. Pupils in a school in Kingston-upon-Thames have worked with their Local Education Business Partnership to set up and run a business, cleaning cars, making and selling sweets and cakes. Through these activities, they are learning to work together well and to make democratic decisions to determine which charities would benefit from the business.

The Eureka Museum in Halifax offers an interesting example of a children's museum which develops a number of positive ways in which children can understand how institutions work. Interactive children's museums of this type are far more developed in the United States, but the Kids' Club Network is working with the government on moving them forward here. They inspire children to learn for themselves in imaginative ways outside class, which is a key attribute for an active and engaged citizenry.

These are examples of developments happening in good schools now, and we need to develop and strengthen them in a variety of different ways. Government should build on all this good practice. However, there are also a number of areas where we must not interfere. It is not the job of government to impose its view of society on pupils. It is not the job of government to dictate precisely what should be taught in schools, and to say, 'This is what a citizen is, according to us, the government'. It is not the job of government to tell schools precisely what approach to take. All of those approaches are dangerous and negative. Some opponents of citizenship education have portrayed various types of society and education system which are dangerous and negative.

It is the job of government, firstly, to provide a framework for citizenship education in schools, to promote coherence and secure entitlement. The Government's proposals for PSHE and Citizenship have been announced as part of the current review of the National

Curriculum; consultation has taken place. The Secretary of State has made the final decisions, and Statutory Orders were laid before Parliament in the autumn.

Secondly, Government should provide practical support and resources for schools, including showing good practice, and we are doing that together with the QCA and others, following consultation on the framework. This is an area where learning from the experience of a wide number of organisations and schools is a real potential strength for the whole education system.

Finally, it is the role of government to listen to children and young people, for example through the Save the Children project based on the UN Convention for the Rights of the Child, or the Children's Parliament on the Environment. We are looking at further ways of doing this as the Citizenship and PSHE curricula are developed.

Citizenship Education attempts to define the conception of the role of the individual in relation to the wider society. There are a number of positive approaches already existing on which we need to build – all with the target of enabling our children and those who follow them to play their role in shaping the society of which they are a part, in an increasingly complex and rapidly changing world.

Endnotes

1 MORI/QCA (1999) *Children's Omnibus Survey* also in *The Guardian* 24.5.99 p1

2 Home Office (1999) *The Stephen Lawrence Inquiry: Report of an Inquiry by Sir William McPherson of Cluny* London: TSO

9. Citizenship: theory into practice

Jenny Talbot

Introduction

Effective practice in teaching Citizenship is largely due to support received from practitioners, students, parents, local government and others. Good ideas alone are not enough. Without input from both end users and the wider community, a good idea is an empty shell. The active involvement of these various constituencies in the development and implementation of citizenship integrates local understanding with expected pedagogical outcomes. The final product is both more comprehensive and more parochial, but parochial in the positive sense in which end users are learning about their own communities. If this foundation is laid securely, Citizenship becomes a subject with growth potential.

Research

The Institute for Citizenship is a non-partisan charitable trust that works to promote informed active citizenship and greater participation in democracy and society. Our research has convinced us of the need for Citizenship resources for schools. In 1996 we commissioned a national survey of the opportunities for citizenship education and community involvement in primary schools.[1] The research revealed the importance that teachers place on citizenship education, and their commitment to it. Teachers expressed a need for advice and guidance, for classroom materials that support active learning and for a greater contribution from other people, including local politicians.

In our recent MORI survey 95 per cent of those questioned agreed with the statement, 'Schools should teach children about how to be a good citizen,' and 66 per cent strongly agreed. Perhaps the strength of feeling here is predicated upon a tacit understanding of the present state of political literacy. Seventy two per cent of those questioned claimed to know just a little or less about their local council. That figure rose to 83 per cent when considering the European Union. Despite this low level of political literacy, 95 per cent of those surveyed considered themselves to be good citizens.[2]

The research indicates both a desire and a need for Citizenship in schools. Anecdotal support for this is strong. In pilot projects introduced by the Institute for Citizenship positive feedback has been strong. Participants gain a new understanding of their connection to local and other levels of government. And that new understanding is usually accompanied by a greater sense of responsibility for what happens in the community.

Effective practice: example 1

Take Your Parent to Vote! was piloted during the recent European Parliament Elections.[3] The project encouraged 7 to 13 year old students to take their parents to vote. Teacher packs were introduced into every school across the Borough of Halton with support materials and lesson plans. Students at Key Stages 2 and 3 learned what the European Parliament is and what it does. They learned what voting is all about and took part in a mock election. And to put all of this both into practice and into context, they were encouraged to take their parents to vote in the recent European Elections.

The object was to use the election to create a relevant learning opportunity in citizenship. The actual turnout on 10 June merely confirmed the need for such work. But the response to this pilot project was very strong. 'The whole experience has certainly raised awareness. The mock election captured the imagination of the pupils' wrote Louise Rees, a teacher at Wade Deacon High School, Widnes.

What made **Take Your Parent to Vote!** interesting was not merely the parental involvement. It was not the huge support it received from local media. It was not even the fact that the LEA was integral to its dissemination. What is surprising here is where the idea came from.

In February 1999 the Institute for Citizenship organised a meeting of local government officers and councillors, representatives from the voluntary sector, local business and the media. The question was put to them, *how can we encourage and inform voter participation at the European Parliament Elections in June?* The seed idea for **Take Your Parent to Vote!** emerged from that meeting. It had full local support from its birth.

Take Your Parent to Vote! will have another pilot opportunity during the election of the Mayor for London and the London Assembly. It will be one of three educational programmes being offered to schools across London under the title of **A Mayor for London – involving student citizens** which has been developed jointly by Arts Inform and the Institute for Citizenship.

Making a difference

Effective practice depends upon support from practitioners, students, parents, local government and others. Good ideas alone are not enough. People need to be involved, encouraged to 'own' the idea or project and to join with others in the development and delivery. Citizenship, perhaps more than any other subject in the curriculum, benefits from the involvement of adults other than teachers. A 'real' local councillor brings participation in local democracy to life for students. A volunteer can relate to students her own story of why volunteering is important, and how it has impacted upon her community.

Often the most important element leading to effective practice is not the project itself but the teacher involved in implementing it. A single highly-motivated teacher can make a dramatic impact upon citizenship in a school. What is more, they very quickly become a real example to students of how one person can make a difference. One of the most important lessons, if any, conveyed by citizenship education is that individuals both singly and collectively can and do make a difference. This lesson has been learnt again and again across the country in schools that have implemented their own citizenship programmes. Almost inevitably there is one enthusiastic teacher who has made the difference.

It is vital that we make an effort to identify the effective practice that is already happening and evolving across the country. Let us not re-invent the wheel. A large amount of effective practice already exists. Once effective practice is identified, it needs to be shared through newsletters, publications, websites and in-service training. We also need a thorough review of literature in order to identify what is already available, to ensure that it is readily accessible and to know what the gaps are in order to fill them.

Many schools have already created a good environment for citizenship. The Institute for Citizenship, in association with the

National Foundation for Educational Research (NFER), is developing a *Citizenship Audit for Schools*.[4] This will aid teachers attempting to assess how well their schools are meeting the Secretary of State's commitment to citizenship. Both teachers and students need to participate in this assessment. It will be a positive step towards a whole school approach to citizenship education.

Effective practice: example 2

It is clear that good ideas become effective practice through the support they gain from practitioners, parents, students and local government. Take, for example, the **Halton Junior Citizenship Project**.[5] This project began as a pilot in six primary schools in Halton. Materials were developed in consultation with teachers. And the pilot was a huge success. However, that was just the beginning. After the pilot the project was thoroughly evaluated with feedback from teachers, from the LEA, and from the children involved.

We listened to what they said. The children thought the materials should include something about the Royal family. They wanted a bound workbook, something they could keep. Teachers wanted greater flexibility, so we introduced discussion photographs. Together we redeveloped the Junior Citizenship Project and introduced it across the entire Borough.

The result is a product in which everyone involved is justly proud. The teachers have confidence in its effectiveness, the local authority knows that it addresses the needs of their community, and the children just love it. The project has now been adopted by 70 per cent of primary schools in Halton.

Relevant resources

Resources for teachers need to be relevant. A host of different learning styles, methods or activities might each be capable of delivering the expected outcomes. But until the fire of the classroom has tested these resources there is no knowing which will go on to become effective practice. The DfEE's introduction of Citizenship into the revised National Curriculum includes a breathing space of two years to develop, collect and share effective practice. We need to spend that time wisely: teachers, parents, school governors, young people and resource providers working together to develop materials that are relevant, user-friendly and fun. Training and support for teachers is crucial to the success of citizenship education.

Effective practice: example 3

At what age can we start Citizenship in schools? The Institute for Citizenship takes the long view on active citizenship. Young people do not become active citizens by accident. Like anything else it has to be learned and practised. The process can even begin in Infant School. In Luton, the Institute piloted the **Infant Citizenship Project** at Key Stage 1. This project is similar in many respects to the Halton Junior Citizenship Project. It builds on that experience and ties its learning outcomes directly to the proposals put forward in the Crick report and reiterated in part in the Secretary of State's proposals. Active citizenship at such a young age is built upon practical experience. For example, young children can develop the habit of participation by learning to care for their environment.[6]

Communication

Citizenship in schools is also about creating opportunities for young people to learn and practise citizenship. We need to encourage young people to speak out on issues they feel are important. Age is no measure of depth of feeling, or the value of a new idea. But speaking out can be difficult. When we share our views with others we risk their disagreement, or worse their failure to understand our point of view. The skill of communicating ideas effectively can be developed through practise.

Effective practice: example 4

In association with Charter 88, the Institute for Citizenship developed and piloted **Active Citizenship Today**, or **ACT!**.[7] This project focuses upon the challenge of communication with students at Key Stage 3. As they write their own press releases and design campaign posters, students experience the power of argument and the persuasiveness of an image. By learning how to communicate our ideas effectively, we gain an appreciation for the ideas that others are trying to communicate to us.

Conclusion

The next two years gives us a unique opportunity to work together in providing resource materials that are relevant, innovative and fun to use. It also gives us time to prepare and support our teachers in the delivery of Citizenship and to explore new and different ways of creating a whole school approach to citizenship. Two years gives us time, but it is not a long time. We all of us need to act now. It is a huge challenge, but in our experience it's a challenge that can be met. There are many willing partners (schools, individual teachers, LEAs and others) keen to make citizenship happen effectively in the classroom and beyond. That willingness and enthusiasm needs to be encouraged and supported, and if we are to share effective practice, co-ordinated too.

Endnotes

1 Kerr, D (1996) *Citizenship Education in Primary Schools Final Report* London: Institute for Citizenship

2 MORI (1998) *Public Attitudes Towards Citizenship* research commissioned by the Institute for Citizenship and NatWest

3 Institute for Citizenship (1999) *Take Your Parents to Vote!* pilot project at Key Stages 2 and 3, London: Institute for Citizenship

4 NFER (1999) *Citizenship Audit for Schools* London: Institute for Citizenship

5 Institute for Citizenship (1999) *Halton Junior Citizenship Project–pupil workbook and teacher pack* London: Institute for Citizenship

6 Institute for Citizenship (1999) *Infant Citizenship Project* London: Institute for Citizenship

7 Charter 88 and Institute for Citizenship (1998) *Active Citizenship Today* London: Institute for Citizenship

For more information on the projects mentioned, as well as new developments in Citizenship resources for schools, contact:

Institute for Citizenship, 62 Marylebone High Street, London W1M 3AF
Tel: 020 7935 4777 Fax: 020 7486 9212 http://www.citizen.org.uk

10. Are schools ready for citizenship education?

William Atkinson

My perspective is firmly grounded in the realities of running an inner city secondary school. It is an interesting school consisting of some 780 students aged 11 to 16. The vast majority of our students arrive at the school with very poor standards of basic numeracy and literacy. Just to give an idea of what I'm talking about, 70 per cent of the current Year 7 students have a reading age of two years or more below their chronological age. Somewhere in the region of 61 per cent feature on the Code of Practice for Special Needs, and many of these pupils have emotional difficulties.

Approximately 65 per cent are entitled to free school meals (the national average is somewhere in the region of 17 per cent). Pupil mobility is one of the major concerns at the school. Within the current Year 11 only 48 per cent of the students started at Phoenix in the September of their Year 7; for Year 10 the figure is 59 per cent, and for Year 9 it is 67 per cent. To these figures needs to be added the 45 per cent of the youngsters in Year 11 who came into the country as refugees or asylum seekers with little or no English.

As someone who has read with great interest the documents on education and citizenship, I find much to support and applaud. I fully share the desire to have citizenship education featured as part of the experiences that are available to all young people in our schools. It is especially important in a school like mine, which caters for students from all over the world – it is a mini 'United Nations'. Citizenship education will help to induct my students into the dominant ways of our society as well as provide knowledge of our various institutions, and in so doing equip them with the necessary knowledge and skills to ensure they are able to play a positive role in adult society. Our democratic way of life calls for knowledge and understanding of our traditions, and above all the desire on the part of the individual to participate.

On the negative side, I am very conscious of the ever-growing demands being made on schools. Recently schools were told that they were responsible for reducing teenage pregnancy. Prior to that announcement we were seen to be in the frontline in the battle against drug abuse, and before that we were informed that schools had a crucial role to play in reducing juvenile crime. In my view it is right that schools should be asked to play their full part in these areas. My concern, however, is with just how much more can we reasonably do and still maintain high quality. We must not forget that we have a duty not only to deliver the national curriculum but also to ensure that every student in our care receives the best possible education and achieves the highest level of attainment.

The notion that teachers only work for 25 to 27 hours per week is pure fiction. The teachers I know on average work an additional 20 to 25 hours running clubs, marking books, revising schemes, attending meetings, meeting parents and most important of all preparing differentiated lessons and materials. Today's schools are highly pressurised places and teachers work far, far in excess of the 27 hours that has been suggested in some quarters as representing a teacher's working week.

Schools, contrary to what some commentators may say, are not resistant to change. Indeed change is something that we encounter on a daily basis, respond positively to and often initiate. Change is an integral part of the learning process.

However, we have to ensure that change is well managed if we are to achieve our desired outcomes. Otherwise, there is a real danger of creating a situation characterised by confusion, overload and ultimately underperformance.

At this moment in time I'm looking in hope to the revised National Curriculum to reduce some of the demands currently made on teachers and thereby create space to accommodate new initiatives. Teachers need to 'feel' that reductions have been made; we need more than mere commitment at the level of language. I have to say that although there are a number of positive developments contained in the new National Curriculum Order, it is not immediately obvious where the cuts have been made. My great fear is that the impact of Citizenship will be diluted and become just one more 'add on' task to be performed. I do not want to see Citizenship go the way of the collective act of worship.

Turning from general observations, I would like to spend a few moments looking at what we at Phoenix High School are currently doing that might come under the umbrella of citizenship education.

The first thing I would say is that we do not have a discrete subject called Citizenship. We do have, however, a set of co-ordinated procedures, policies, and activities that contain many of the elements of citizenship. These include:

- a written set of rules which stipulates what is expected of students from the moment they leave home in the morning for school until they return home after school
- an explicit value system, which makes clear that, everyone is of equal worth irrespective of ability, race, gender etc
- personal, social and health education programmes for all years
- a reward system that explicitly seeks out and celebrates success wherever it can be found
- a Code of Expectation, which provides students and parents with guidance on teaching and classroom organisation
- a set of sanctions and related procedures which apply throughout the school
- an appeals procedure for students and parents
- a school council comprising of representatives from each tutor group
- a prefect system drawn from Year 11 students
- a two-week work experience programme for all Year 10 students
- year and school assemblies used to reinforce key values and beliefs
- work with various charities

We believe that the work we are doing in this area not only allows our students to develop an understanding of their rights, responsibilities and opportunities, but also their place in the wider community.

In our view this work is crucial in creating a sense of shared identity and purpose at a time when there is so much conflict and intolerance in our communities. A recent Ofsted report made a number of observations, which underscore the positive impact of these activities:

- 'The provision for spiritual development is good. Pupils experience collective worship in assemblies twice a week. The assemblies are of high quality. They communicate a strong message that staff apply to the circumstance of each individual. There are opportunities for quiet reflection on the deepest issues that life raises! Although the assembly themes are broadly Christian, the appreciation of other faith cultures is encouraged. Pupils and staff take part in assemblies, and celebrate pupils' achievements and staff use information on events to promote the mission of the school.

- 'Provision for moral development is very good. There is a clear Code of Conduct, and staff both enforce and promote the code in lessons in and around the school. A sensible system of rewards and sanctions continues the message. In such subjects as Personal and Social Education, English, History, Geography and Religious Education, teachers and pupils discuss moral issues in depth, and staff encourage pupils to apply their learning to their own lives. The school gives a very clear message as to what is wrong and what is right and what making moral decisions means and involves.

- 'Provision for social development is very good. The school community provides a very good example of the importance of an orderly society. Permanent staff provide good role models, and they expect pupils to reflect their example in the way they behave. The school is a fair and just community and this helps pupils learn to value justice.

- 'The school recognises and celebrates the achievements of pupils outside of school, and promotes the local community it serves as a society of opportunity and rich variety'.[1]

It is important to note that there are many schools at both primary and secondary level which are doing more than Phoenix High School. Our ability to continue working effectively depends on how we cope with ever growing demands made on us and the level and quality of resources at our disposal. I am very worried that unless concessions are made, the commitment that currently exists in many schools to support citizenship education could be undermined. There is a real danger that we could generate a great deal of activity, which produces very little productively. We must aim at all times for quality.

In conclusion I would plead with the gatekeepers to see the National Curriculum as a whole, and appreciate that the vast majority of schools are already working flat out with little or no spare capacity to 'add on' without 'taking away'. Above all, we need to keep at the forefront of our minds the fact that teachers have a right to a life outside school. Already difficulties in recruitment and retention in certain areas of the country, and certain curriculum subjects, make it impossible to deliver aspects of the current National Curriculum properly.

Endnote

1 Ofsted (1999) *Report of the Inspection of Phoenix High School* London: Ofsted

11. Key assessment issues

Martin Cross

Introduction

Why do we need citizenship education? Other contributions to this book deal more directly with that question, but a straightforward and convincing answer can be found in a series of seminal reports prepared by Valerie Bayliss for the RSA:

- *Redefining Work,* which outlined the way in which working life has changed and is continuing to change, and the need for education for young people and adults to alter to meet the new challenges[1]
- *Redefining Schooling,* which analysed the way in which schooling structures and approaches are not geared to the changed needs of the present and the future[2]
- *Opening Minds,* which suggested a redefinition of the curriculum to meet those changes and challenges. One of the five main pillars of that redefined curriculum would be 'Competencies for Citizenship'.[3]

At the same time the Secretary of State has been considering how to approach the required review of the National Curriculum, against a background where he had accepted as a main priority the need to maintain stability for schools. He nevertheless accepted the arguments for the importance of modernising the curriculum, first by establishing the Advisory Group on *Education for Citizenship and the Teaching of Democracy* in schools chaired by Professor Bernard Crick[4] and then by building on that Group's recommendations when publishing his proposals for a revised National Curriculum.[5]

This chapter accepts the centrality of citizenship to appropriate educational arrangements for the future, both for those at school and for those over 16. It then addresses directly the questions as to why and how assessment can and should be integral to the successful introduction of citizenship education.

Assessment for what?

Assessment has a number of purposes. We will need to be clear as to which of those are relevant, bearing in mind particularly that it is difficult for any one assessment instrument to serve more than a single purpose.

Assessment can be a direct aid to teaching and learning, that is, it can serve a *formative* purpose. Such assessment is diagnostic and should form part of all learning programmes. Assessment of this kind can help both the learner and the teacher to judge the extent to which learning has taken place, and to focus on those outcomes where more needs to be done. Judgements about effort and progress are intrinsic to it in each individual case, in a way that would not be appropriate in assessments for other purposes.

Secondly, assessment can take place as a means of asserting *public accountability*, to judge the effectiveness of the school and of the teachers. Such assessment can often take place at a fairly generalised level, and is concerned with issues of comparability and norm-referenced benchmarks. This approach has become familiar to us in recent years with its use for performance and league tables of schools. It tells us comparatively little in respect of the individual pupil.

Thirdly, assessment can be *summative*: recognising an individual's achievement, often for certification purposes. This type of assessment may be reported in a relatively detailed way, 'profiling' achievement across a range of activities, or may be reported by a summary grade, for which a grade descriptor (unknown to most users) will exist indicating the typical profile of achievement required for that grade. Effort and progress are not relevant to certificated assessment, which is a statement of capability against required outcomes. This type of assessment is particularly important for progression purposes and may be used by gatekeepers (admissions tutors, personnel departments) for selection to further and higher education programmes and to employment.

Implications for citizenship education in schools

In the context of the different purposes of assessment, then, what needs to be done in our schools? The Crick report *Education for Citizenship and the Teaching of Democracy in Schools* proposed a framework of learning outcomes across the key stages. The Secretary of State's recent proposals, in reviewing the National Curriculum, build on that framework by proposing non-statutory guidelines for Key Stages 1 and 2, and statutory programmes of study and attainment targets for Key Stages 3 and 4.

These arrangements will certainly provide a basis for *formative* assessment. Schools and teachers will have a clear indication of what should be taught and learned in each key stage, thus enabling them to track individual progress and provide feedback to pupils. Equally, they will have a framework against which to report on pupils' progress to parents through the individual's annual report and through parents' evenings.

In terms of *public accountability*, the governors can use the framework as a template for judging the effectiveness of the school's approach to citizenship education, and for reporting on that to parents as a whole through the annual governors' report. Beyond this, Ofsted should now review its 'Framework for Inspection' to take account of the revised National Curriculum and to enable inspectors to focus more specifically on the effectiveness of schools in delivering the new requirements. They will then be able to judge quality, and to benchmark within and across schools, reporting both to institutions and more publicly.

Summative assessment within schools is essentially an issue only for Key Stage 4. Pupils' achievements in this particular Key Stage, in National Curriculum and any other subjects they may be studying, are typically assessed for certification purposes through the GCSE. If summative assessment is thought valuable or even essential at the end of compulsory schooling, then it is difficult to see why it should not be applied across *all* curriculum subjects. The following section explores this area further.

Status and qualifications

From the age of 14 and on into post-compulsory education, pupils and students are, and expect to be, subject to the assessment and certification of the outcomes of their learning, of their achievements. Assessment and certification are of fundamental importance, therefore, not only intrinsically and in a pedagogical sense but also in terms of the perceived status and importance attached to particular areas of study.

It is not a new insight to state 'that which is assessed is that which gets taught' or, more bluntly, 'if it's not assessed, then it won't be taught'. It may not be new, but we constantly need to remind ourselves that it is so, and that we should react accordingly. Citizenship education could be said to be required by the 1988 Education Reform Act and exemplified among the cross-curricular themes promoted by the National Curriculum Council in its guidance on implementing that Act. Yet, because the statutory assessment arrangements detail other subjects and make no reference to Citizenship, we find that Citizenship plays little part in the curriculum for most students in Key Stage 4 and beyond.

This question of status is further reinforced through the British emphasis on national qualifications. Where Citizenship activity does take place, it is likely to be mentioned within an individual's Record of Achievement. Yet an employer, or an FHE institution, may pay little regard to this in practice, preferring instead to concentrate on the achievements authenticated by a national body, such as GCSEs, A levels, GNVQs or whatever. It is these qualifications, too, on which the media will focus every summer, reinforcing the message that these and these alone are what matter. And Citizenship is not there as yet.

Consider further the resourcing and reward mechanisms for schools and colleges. Within both the state and independent sectors, financial viability and success depend upon parental demand for places for their children. There is no doubt that a significant driver of that demand is comparative achievement by institutions in the performance tables, based on qualifications. Curriculum activity which does not lead to a qualification and therefore cannot contribute to performance tables tends to be ruthlessly discarded. Within further education the funding mechanism (one which may soon be extended more widely within post-16 education) relates directly to programmes leading to nationally recognised qualifications, with an element rewarding achievement within these qualifications as well.

Against this cultural, status and reward background can there be any doubt that, if citizenship education is to be valued or indeed happen at all, it must lead to certification and qualifications, with their concomitant requirements for valid and reliable assessment?

Implications for citizenship education post-16

While many of the points made in the previous section could be applied to post-16 as well as pre-16 citizenship education, the first sections of this chapter have concentrated on schools pre-16. The justification for this is that the compulsory phase of education is subject to statute in a way that the post-compulsory phase is not: the National Curriculum, Ofsted inspection arrangements and so on.

But, as the Crick report said, 'Preparation for citizenship clearly cannot end at age 16 just as young people begin to have more access to the opportunities, rights and responsibilities of adult citizenship amid the world of work.'[6] Schools, colleges and other training providers vary considerably in the extent to which they make 'enrichment' activities – which may include citizenship education – available to their post-16 students. For full-time students, provision of enrichment activities varies from the poor to the very good. For part-time students, however, virtually no enrichment activities are provided at all. European commentators are always struck, for instance, by the way in which UK programmes leading to vocational qualifications are narrowly instrumental, with no connections to the wider economic and societal aspects of working life.

This chapter on Assessment may not be the place to consider the broader case for citizenship education post-16, but it does need to take account of some clear and welcome trends in Government policy. From September 2000, the Qualifying for Success reforms will be introduced, which aim to encourage young people to pursue a broader post-16 curriculum. The Further Education Funding Council (FEFC) has announced that, to facilitate this aim, it will revise its funding arrangements to support a new *minimum curriculum entitlement* for all full-time 16 to 19 year old students. As well as covering A levels, GNVQs, vocational programmes and key skills 'this will also include vital enrichment studies, to enable young people to develop as adults and citizens and cope with the demands of society in the 21st century'.[7]

From 2001 the work of the FEFC, of the Training and Enterprise Councils and certain Local Education Authority work will be brought together in a new national Learning and Skills Council (LSC). The LSC will thus have a much wider and more comprehensive brief than its predecessors to engender a culture of lifelong learning which, in David

Blunkett's words, 'contributes to sustaining a civilised and cohesive society in which people develop as active citizens...'. Alongside this, new inspection arrangements will be created to reduce the confusion and overlap between the current three post-16 inspectorates: Ofsted, the FEFC Inspectorate, and the Training Standards Council Inspectorate.

Still more recently, the Cabinet Office Social Exclusion Unit has produced its report 'Bridging the Gap'.[8] Launched by the Prime Minister and David Blunkett, a key action is that the DfEE will commission the QCA to consult on proposals for a common 'graduation certificate' for all to aim for by the age of 19. At Level 2, this would include 'mainstream' qualifications, key skills and curriculum enrichment and community participation. The last would offer 'recognition for community and citizenship activities ... in line with Government policy'.[9] Over the last year, too, QCA has been undertaking a feasibility study into the prospects for an overarching certificate at Level 3: this too might include a requirement for enrichment activities such as Citizenship.

Assessment post-16

Given these possible developments, what are the implications for the assessment of Citizenship post-16?

First of all, as the Crick report suggested, there will be a need to develop a coherent framework of learning outcomes, building on the pre-16 experience and capable of application to the very wide range and diversity of post-16 education and training. Accompanying that framework, there will need to be guidance as to the minimum entitlement either for all 16-19 year olds or at least those in full-time education. This would acknowledge that the latter are pursuing co-ordinated programmes, while adults engaged in learning may choose a much more limited or eclectic menu to suit their particular needs.

Once such a framework and guidance exists, *formative* assessment then has a context within which it can operate in the normal way, as suggested earlier in relation to pre-16 education. The framework would also enable the new post-16 inspectorate(s) to include this area in their inspection requirements and arrangements, thus addressing the *public accountability* issue. For *summative* assessment purposes, qualifications or more probably unit certificates would need to be developed, within the National Qualifications Framework, relating to the learning outcomes. Earlier sections make the case as to why summative assessment should lead to certification, and those arguments are reinforced post-16 by the recent Government policy announcements.

Certificated assessment

What are the principal technical issues that need addressing in respect of assessment and certification?

- At Key Stage 4, for reasons advanced earlier, assessment should lead to certification either as a GCSE or, more probably, as a 'short course' GCSE. The latter would perhaps be more realistic in terms of its demands on curriculum time for all pupils. Interestingly, this route has proved successful in respect of another subject required by law, which has not usually been certificated in the past: Religious Education.

  Post-16, bearing in mind the diverse nature of students and their programmes, a unit-based approach is likely to be more appropriate. OCR has been working on such an approach with the Coalition for Citizenship, which brings together the Council for Education in World Citizenship, the Citizenship Foundation, Community Service Volunteers, the Institute for Citizenship Studies, and the Centre for Citizenship Studies in Education (Leicester University). Units, to be available at Levels 1-3 of the National Qualifications Framework, might be:
  - Citizens' Rights and Responsibilities in the Community
  - The Individual in Society
  - Citizenship in Action

  Units could be certificated individually, could be combined to create a three-unit citizenship qualification, or could be combined with other units from a suite also relating to, for example, Careers Education, Work/Community Experience, Employability, PSHE. Such units and qualifications could also be available, as an alternative to the GCSE route, in Key Stage 4 where they might be particularly attractive to those able to plan a progressive 14-19 curriculum including credit accumulation.

- GCSEs, at least, involve the grading of performance (and any certification necessarily involves concepts of success and failure). Some seem uncomfortable with these ideas in relation to Citizenship, but a little reflection would suggest that matters are not so problematic. An analogy could be Religious Education: students are not labelled as sinners or moral and spiritual failures if they do not achieve high grades in a RE GCSE examination. Other subjects that we routinely assess, grade and certificate are as essential for successful adult life as Citizenship. Communication and literacy are vital, for instance, but we have no particular problem with the concept of awarding a low grade in GCSE English. Why should Citizenship be any different? What we should not expect, however, is failure: we should be looking for our schools to produce knowledgeable and effective citizens, just as we expect them to ensure that their pupils leave with the required standards of literacy and numeracy.

- Given the pressures on curriculum time, there is rightly an interest in the question as to whether other subjects can contribute to the coverage of the knowledge and understanding required within Citizenship, and whether their assessment could meet the assessment requirements for citizenship. On the first, it is clearly possible to identify or construct overlaps with subjects such as GCSE Humanities or A level General Studies. The Crick report also outlines the way in which teaching and learning in subjects such as History, Geography and English can contribute to coverage of elements of Citizenship. Within a revised National Curriculum, these opportunities could be emphasised by some rewriting to use common terminology and by 'mapping' outcomes across subjects. On the second, it would be technically possible for one piece of work to cover the assessment objectives for more than one certificated subject, although QCA regulations may discourage or prevent this.

  By analogy with the key skills, however, a process of 'signposting' possibilities for links with Citizenship in the syllabus specifications for other subjects should prove helpful. Citizenship itself should provide an ideal context for the development and achievement of the six key skills: Communication, Application of Number, Information Technology, Working with Others, Improving own Learning and Performance, and Problem Solving. It might be particularly helpful to note that IT in particular will provide many opportunities to develop skills, knowledge and understanding in citizenship.

- Assessment of citizenship outcomes must be both valid and reliable. An analysis of the outcomes indicates that those requirements necessitate a range of assessment methodologies. Some of these will of necessity be activity- or experience-based, while others will be appropriate to a more conventional written examination.

  For example, the draft attainment target at Key Stage 4 includes: 'Pupils show a comprehensive knowledge and understanding of those topical events which are studied, the rights, responsibilities and duties of citizens, the role of the voluntary sector, forms of government, the criminal justice, legal and economic systems, locally, nationally and internationally.'[10] This can readily be assessed through the externally set end of course examination that QCA criteria require for GCSE.

  The draft target also includes:

  'Pupils participate effectively in school and community-based activities, demonstrating a willingness and commitment to evaluate critically such activity.'[11] This will need to be assessed through practical and project- or assignment-based approaches, with strands of competence identified for assessment against defined criteria. Much good practice of this type of assessment has been developed in General National Vocational Qualifications (GNVQs), for instance.

  The unit-based approach for post-16 qualifications would enable greater weight to be placed on the practical elements, if appropriate, given the greater opportunities available to adults than to school children in terms of community activity.

Conclusion

This contribution has only been able to skim the surface of some complex issues. The fundamental principles are clear, however:

- working life in all its aspects continues to change
- 'citizenship' is an essential part of making sense of, and a success of, working life
- Citizenship must therefore be a crucial element of our curriculum provision
- assessment of achievement in Citizenship facilitates, motivates and provides accountability.

Endnotes

1 Bayliss, V (1998) *Redefining Work* London: Royal Society of Arts

2 Bayliss, V (1998) *Redefining Schooling* London: Royal Society of Arts

3 Bayliss, V (1999) *Opening Minds* London: Royal Society of Arts

4 Advisory Group on Citizenship (1998) *Education for Citizenship and the teaching of democracy in schools* London: Qualifications and Curriculum Authority

5 QCA/DfEE (1999) *The review of the National Curriculum in England – the Secretary of State's proposals* London: Qualifications and Curriculum Authority

6 Advisory Group on Citizenship (1998) *op cit* p12

7 Further Education Funding Council Circular 33/99

8 Social Exclusion Unit (1999) *Bridging the Gap: New Opportunities for 16-18 Year Olds not in Education, Employment or Training* London: TSO

9 *ibid* p68

10 QCA/DfEE (1999) *op cit* p31

11 *ibid* p31